BEING HAPPY

(Even When You Don't Get What You Want)

BEING HAPPY

(Even When You Don't Get What You Want)

The Truth About
Manifesting and Desire

GINA LAKE

Endless Satsang Foundation

www.RadicalHappiness.com

This book was formerly titled *Anatomy of Desire: How to Be Happy Even When You Don't Get What You Want*

Cover photograph: © Chernishev Maksim/Dreamstime.com

ISBN: 978-1544781082

CONTENTS

CHAPTER SIX

INTRODUCTION

Desire is such a juicy subject. We love desiring and we hate desiring. It drives us and it drives us crazy. We want to be rid of it and we don't. We are as conflicted about desiring as we are about our desires: We want something, and then we want the opposite. One thing we know for sure is that we want. Wanting is so much a part of being human that we can't imagine life without it.

And yet wanting causes us a lot of suffering: We suffer over not having what we want, not getting what we want, not knowing what we want, and wanting opposite things. When we get what we want, we even suffer over that, as we discover that it doesn't meet our hopes and expectations.

We put a lot of energy into wanting, and we have a lot of expectations that getting what we want will finally make us happy. But what we find is that getting what we want mostly just leads to wanting more or wanting something different. We are never done with wanting. It's like an itch that is never satisfied. So while we have great hopes that our desires will bring us happiness, that is not our experience.

Our desires toss us to and fro until we tire of that and begin to question the purpose and value of desiring. We become more interested in mastering our desires than getting them met because we see their falseness and the suffering they cause. We see that maybe our desires aren't worthy motivators or trustworthy guides for where to put our energy.

This book won't necessarily help you get what you want, but it will help you want what you get. It will help you understand desire and its purpose in your life. It will help you discriminate between your Heart's desires and the ego's, and it will help you relate to your ego's desires in a way that reduces suffering and increases joy. By pointing out the myths about desire that keep us tied to our ego's desires and the suffering they cause, it will help you be happy regardless of your desires and whether you are attaining them. So it is also about spiritual freedom, or liberation, which comes from letting your Heart guide you instead of the ego's desires. It's ultimately about becoming a lover of life instead of a desirer.

CHAPTER 1

The Fundamentals of Desire

Desire Is Not the Problem

Desire is the cause of suffering, says the Buddha. So to stop suffering, it seems that we need to stop desiring. But if desiring is something we need to stop doing, why is it so much a part of our nature? Is this some kind of cruel joke that, in every moment, we desire something, and yet that desire is the source of our suffering?

Looking at it this way, desire seems like a problem, but really the only problem is that we suffer over our desires. It's possible to desire without suffering, which is fortunate, because desires are not under our control. They arise and then disappear, like every other thought, and we are not in control of our thoughts. They arise out of nowhere and disappear just as mysteriously and unpredictably. We are not responsible for having thoughts and desires, but what we do about them makes the difference between happiness and suffering. And that is what we are responsible for. That is where we have a choice.

For example, the desire for a new car arises. What do you do with that? Some buy a new car, some buy a used one, some steal one, some fantasize about one, some feel bad because they don't have one, and some ignore the desire. Each of these choices has a very different outcome and results in a very different experience. Some of these choices, such as stealing a car, can even alter the course of your life. Desires, alone, are not powerful, since they are just thoughts and can't, by themselves, affect reality. But what we choose to do about our desires can and does affect reality, and certainly our experience of it.

The Components of Desire

The desire for something like a car has the same structure, anatomy, as every other desire, and it can be dissected and understood. Understanding the anatomy of desire can bring some freedom from desire, that is, freedom from the need to have a specific desire met. While there is no freedom from desiring, because desiring will exist as long as we are human, it is possible to become free from needing to have our desires met. For that, we need to look more closely at what a desire is composed of.

The most obvious component of desire is thought. Desire is a thought. It's the thought, "I want...." But desire is also more than just this thought. It's a special kind of thought that has the power to move us because that thought becomes associated with emotions, the second component of desire, and also with drive, the third component, which has the potential to result in action. Desire is a particular kind of thought that is more compelling than most other thoughts because it has emotions and drive attached to it.

The emotions attached to a desire vary from fear to exhilaration and can be a mixture of many different emotions as well. For instance, consider the desire for a car: We want cars for all sorts of reasons: to go places, for fun, to impress people, to pick up things, to feel safe. Cars provide us with lots of benefits. The thought of having these benefits or not having these benefits results in emotions: When we think of having fun in a car, we feel happy; when we think of not being safe because we don't have a safe car, we feel scared. The desire for a car evokes certain emotions, and then trying to manage those emotions becomes a driving force: Actions are taken to try to get the emotions we want, such as fun, and avoid the ones we don't want, such as fear.

The emotions that have been stirred up by desiring are often pumped up with other thoughts (e.g., "I need to have this or else...."), and those thoughts result in more emotions and drives, which are out of proportion to the desired object or experience. If you invest a desire with the belief that your happiness or survival depends on it, that desire can balloon into something that consumes you. We tend to tell stories about our desires that make our desires feel more important than they are. The emotions that result from those stories make the desire feel real, as if that desire is more than just a thought.

The most powerful desires are those we believe will fulfill our basic human needs to survive and be loved. The drive to be loved is actually related to the drive to survive: We want to be loved because being loved is likely to help us survive. Every desire can be boiled down to the most basic desire: the desire to survive.

Another basic drive is to be happy. Once our survival is not at stake, the desire to be happy becomes the primary drive. We have many ideas about what we need to be happy. We pursue those things we think will make us happy, and doing that structures our lives and determines our activities because we believe that fulfilling those desires will result in finally being happy. Here is an exercise that will help you become more aware of what you desire and what you tell yourself about your desires:

Exercise: Exploring Your Desires

What do you desire? Name one thing you desire. Notice the feelings that accompany that desire. They are probably a mixture of longing, exhilaration, fear, and sadness. What are the ideas you hold about that desire that create those feelings? Make a list of all them. How important does that desire feel? What do you tell yourself that makes that desire feel true and important?

Examining your desires this way will help put them in perspective. The truth is there isn't a single desire you can name that your happiness depends on.

The Source of Happiness

There are two kinds of happiness: that which comes and goes and that which is forever present and untouched by circumstances. The happiness that comes and goes is the happiness we experience when we achieve our desires. The happiness that is ever-present, on the other hand, isn't dependent on achieving anything because that happiness is our true nature. At our deepest core is happiness, peace, and contentment. We don't have to go searching for happiness because we already have it—we *are* it.

The problem is the ego doesn't realize this great truth. The ego believes it needs things and experiences to be happy, so that's what it pursues. It generates desires (thoughts), which generate emotions, which generate actions, and life moves forward accordingly. Most people's actions and reactions are based on their desires, on thoughts generated by the ego, which, in turn evoke emotions, more thoughts, and more emotions.

The fact that our lives are driven by desires is not wrong or a mistake. We are meant to have the lives we are having, which are full of experience. The Divine loves the experience it is having through each of us. It welcomes every experience, even the painful and difficult ones, simply because the Divine loves experience. You can feel this love for experience when your mind is quiet and you tune into the Divine within you, which will be referred to here as *Essence*. When we are in touch with Essence, we feel the joy of just being and experiencing. The reason it is possible to be happy regardless of our circumstances is because the real you, Essence, is supremely happy regardless of circumstances.

The only reason we aren't happy with something about ourselves or our life is because we have told ourselves a story about life that is making us unhappy. Instead of blaming the story for our unhappiness, we blame the circumstances, as if it is impossible for us to be happy within those circumstances, which is a lie. It's always possible for us to be happy. In fact, it's impossible for Essence to be unhappy.

Nothing can change this happiness, which can be experienced very subtly energetically as a hum inside. It's like an inner smile. In every moment, regardless of what is happening, something inside you is smiling. This something is the real you: Essence.

Ego and Essence

The part of us we are most familiar with is the false self, and it's happy only when its desires are being met, and then only fleetingly. It's who we think of ourselves as. That part of us will be referred to as the *egoic self* or the *ego*. And since part of the mind is used by the ego, and the mind is how the ego expresses itself, that aspect of the mind will be referred to as the *egoic mind*. We experience the ego, or the egoic mind, as a voice in our head that speaks to us as if it is our own or someone else's voice, commenting about life.

Every idea we have about ourselves makes up our ego. The ego is truly a figment of the imagination, or mind, because it's nothing but the thoughts we have about ourselves. The ego thinks itself into existence. The thoughts the ego has about itself define it and give it a kind of reality so that we actually think of ourselves as the *I*. But this *I* has no reality apart from the mind. It may seem like other people relate to the *I*, but in fact, they are relating to their own ideas about us, which are equally imaginary.

The real you (Essence) exists beyond all thoughts, all feelings, and anything that can be sensed. Essence can't be understood with the mind, described by the mind, or sensed with our usual senses. And yet we are all so familiar with Essence that we overlook it, like the air that surrounds and sustains us but is barely noticed. The real you is overshadowed by the loud and noisy egoic mind, which convinces us that thoughts *about* ourselves are who we are.

The real you is intangible. Because it's not a thing, the real you is often referred to as Nothing, or Nothingness. And yet there is an energetic sensation and other clues associated with the experience of the real you that give it away. Who we really are, Essence, can be felt energetically as a sense of aliveness. However, if we are attending to anything else, we aren't likely to notice that aliveness because it is a much subtler experience than our thoughts or sensory experience.

Although Essence is barely perceptible, it is what has been

living your life in cooperation with your ego and mind. Essence allows the egoic mind to rule and shape our choices, while Essence continues to try to influence us in other ways. The real you, Essence, has intentions for us and this life, which are often unlike those of the ego and may even be in contradiction to it.

Occasionally Essence conveys its intentions through the mind, but usually it conveys them through our intuition and the intuition of others, whom it uses as mouthpieces. Essence's intentions are delivered repeatedly until they are received. However, Essence can't force us to follow its suggestions. It allows us to choose between following the thoughts and desires that arise from the ego or following our intuition and the spontaneous urges to act that come from Essence.

Essence expresses itself not only through intuition, but also through urges to take action: We feel moved to do or say something, and we do it. Whenever we act spontaneously in this way, it is likely to be Essence acting and speaking through us. When the ego acts and speaks through us, the actions and speech are often more calculated and thought about and less spontaneous. Spontaneity that is free of thought and which feels right and uplifting is the mark of Essence. When our actions and speech are aligned with Essence in this way, we naturally feel happy because happiness is a quality of Essence. This happiness is simple, pure, and deeply fulfilling. It can be felt whenever we touch into Essence.

It is always possible to experience Essence, because there is nothing closer to us than Essence. We are Essence, and it awaits our notice of it and rejoices in our awareness of it. Who is the *you*, then, that has to become aware of the real you? This *you* is the sense of being an individual who is separate from others. In reality, there is only one Being here. Imagine that—everything that exists, has ever existed, and will ever exist is the expression of one Being!

You are an expression of the One Being, who is enjoying this and every other expression for the uniqueness, beauty, depth, and experience these expressions bring to it. The One Being that you are is supremely happy with you and with every one of its expressions, regardless of the choices they make, because every choice leads to experience, and experience is the purpose of creation. From the perspective of the One Being, there are no wrong choices.

This is a very different perspective than our egos have. The ego is forever evaluating choices, possibilities, and experiences and forming opinions and preferences. Those opinions and preferences are behind many of our desires: We want a new car because we prefer a new car over an old one. We have this preference because we have an opinion that new cars are better than old ones. Although it may be true that a new car performs and looks better than an old one, it isn't true that a new car increases our ability to be safer or happier, which is often the assumption, or the story, we tell ourselves. That story turns our preferences and opinions into a desire.

Safety and happiness can't be achieved through having, only through *being*. When we are in touch with Essence, we are happy, and fears about safety or anything else dissolve in the face of the immensity of who we are. What could happen that the immensity that we are couldn't handle? It knows how to enjoy every experience, not just the pleasant and easy ones. Furthermore, it loves the learning and growth that come from challenging experiences, and so do we when we are in touch with Essence.

We Are Evolving Toward Greater Love

The good news is that every experience results in evolution. That evolution is an evolution toward greater goodness and love, and it leads, eventually, to a return to the Oneness that we are. This truth may be difficult to see at times, but that doesn't mean it isn't true. Every experience serves growth and is welcomed by the Divine, who has designed us to evolve in just the way we do: through challenges and by becoming lost in the illusion of a separate self.

It's no mistake that you think of yourself as you do, as an individual with certain beliefs, opinions, thoughts, desires, memories, dreams, feelings, fantasies, roles, and a certain history. Those ideas make up your identity, or how you describe yourself. They seem like who you are. However, they are just a set of ideas you believe about yourself. Such ideas are how we distinguish ourselves from one another: "I am someone who..., and you are someone who...." These distinctions and differences are necessary to make the world go around. They make life interesting and challenging. They create experience. Without these differences, the Divine couldn't have the experiences it has through us.

The Divine *is* us, and it created us for the purpose of experience. However, for the Divine to have experiences through us, we have to forget that we are the Divine. This is accomplished by giving each of us an ego, which provides the sense that we are separate individuals. This illusion of separation allows the Divine to have a variety of experiences. Because everyone is unique and because no situation can ever be replicated, the possibilities for experience are endless.

Pure experience isn't the Divine's only intention. The Divine also intends for us to evolve and for us to come to know our true nature. We begin our incarnations lost and cut off from our true nature and expressing qualities opposite it. Fear runs us rather than love. As we evolve, we learn to overcome fear and express more love. Fear is the emotion that is most representative of the ego and of being cut off from our true nature, while love is most representative of our true nature. So we are evolving from being identified with the ego and fear to being identified with Essence and love. This evolution is slow and gradual, and it takes many incarnations and entails all kinds of experiences.

At a certain point in our evolution, we begin to spend more time identified with Essence and less time identified with the ego, and our words and actions express Essence more than they express the ego. You are undoubtedly at this point, or you wouldn't be taking the time to read this. At a certain point in our evolution, the desire to awaken to our true nature becomes a driving force that can't be denied, and awakening happens.

The desire to awaken out of the ego, the false self, and to know and express our true nature begins to override the drive to fulfill the ego's desires because those desires have proven to be disappointing. When we have finally had our fill of seeking happiness in ways that don't satisfy us, by going after what the ego wants, we seek a deeper, more real, and long-lasting happiness. That happiness comes from contact with Essence.

Initially, the desire to awaken may be more of a desire to stop suffering, since suffering is often what spurs us on in our evolution. Then as we begin to experience Essence more, we lose our attraction to the ego's world and what it has to offer, and we choose to be aligned with Essence more often. Choosing Essence is simply a matter of putting our attention on Essence's qualities—love, peace, joy, acceptance, and contentment— instead of on the ego (the *I*), its thoughts, desires, fantasies, beliefs, opinions, and the feelings that arise from them.

Desires That Come from Essence

This brings us to an important point: There are desires that come from the ego and desires, or intentions, that come from Essence. They are experienced similarly, as drives to do or say something that will help achieve that desire or intention. The main difference is that the ego tells stories about its desires and fuels them with emotions (e.g., "When I get this, everyone will look up to me"), while Essence simply moves us to do or say something that will bring about its intentions. When we are aligned with Essence, our actions and speech feel clear and clean, and they lead to the intended result, while listening to the egoic mind often leaves us feeling confused and conflicted about what we want and how to get what we want.

The other most obvious difference is that getting what the ego wants brings only brief satisfaction and happiness, while getting what Essence wants brings deep happiness and fulfillment. You know when you are aligned with Essence's intentions by feelings of excitement, joy, fulfillment, peace, relaxation, and contentment. These same feelings may be present when the ego gets what it wants, but they are more like a lower octave of the feelings that arise from Essence, and they don't last.

The desires, or intentions, of Essence aren't like the ego's desires, which usually relate to enhancing the ego's sense of safety, security, and superiority in the world. Rather, Essence desires, or intends, that we express more of the qualities of our true nature. It intends that we become more loving, accepting, wise, understanding, peaceful, and compassionate. It also intends that we fulfill a particular goal for this incarnation, which was decided before birth.

That goal is not spelled out specifically before birth, nor is it known exactly how or if it will be achieved, or how it will unfold. All of this remains to be seen and depends to a great extent on our choices and the choices of others who are involved with us. Nevertheless, before every incarnation, we set out to accomplish something that will promote our evolution and the evolution of others. That goal is often referred to as the *life task* or *life purpose.*

The life purpose is achieved by following inner drives that come from Essence. Every day, we experience drives from Essence that serve Essence's goals and also unfold our life in ordinary ways. Essence moves us not only to fulfill our life purpose, but also to feed ourselves and take care of other basic needs necessary for our survival and happiness. It moves us to go to the store, get an education, eat properly, develop our talents, make friends, and do other things to support ourselves and others in the world and to flourish physically, emotionally, intellectually, and spiritually.

The ego is also concerned with our survival, growth, and happiness. The difference is, the ego doesn't know how to best achieve these things, while Essence does. So following our ego's thoughts won't have the same result as following Essence's nudges. For instance, the ego might encourage you to work at a job that pays your bills but isn't fulfilling. Essence is better able to lead you to meaningful work and ways of supporting yourself that fit your particular personality, strengths, and life purpose. Fulfillment is important to Essence and less important to the ego, which is more concerned about security, appearances, and amassing more money, things, and knowledge in its attempt to be superior to others.

Essence drives us through urges to act and speak, while the

ego drives us with desires, which are thoughts pumped up by emotions (e.g., "I have to have this or else...."). The ego uses fear to inspire us to take action, while Essence inspires us through feelings of joy, excitement, happiness, and elation. When we feel those feelings, that is Essence encouraging us to take action in a particular direction. When we don't feel those feelings or when we feel the opposite ones — sadness, depression, and anger — that's a sign we are following the ego's dictates instead of Essence's intentions.

Following the ego may result in achievements, but those achievements may not result in happiness and fulfillment because the ego doesn't seek fulfillment as much as it seeks achievements and accumulation of wealth, prestige, security, and knowledge. The ego believes that what it seeks will bring it the happiness it desires, but it's wrong. Only by following Essence's intentions will we find the true happiness and fulfillment we are looking for.

Pursuing the Ego's Desires

The ego is rarely happy because it tends to want more or better than whatever is showing up in the moment, and it wants what it wants now. The moment is rarely good enough for the ego. If, by chance, the ego is happy with what is showing up, it draws us away from the experience of happiness with concerns about losing what it likes or with schemes for holding onto what it likes. By doing this, the ego cuts short the brief experiences of happiness it does have. So even when the ego does experience happiness as a result of attaining its goals, it quickly spoils that happiness with worries and other thoughts that interfere with feeling happy.

The ego just doesn't know how to be happy. It doesn't know

what we need to be happy, it goes after the wrong things, and it spoils the experience of happiness when it does finally get it. And yet we believe that pursuing the ego's ideas about what will make us happy will make us happy, and if doing so isn't working now, it will work someday. We keep pursuing the ego's desires, even though they have proven repeatedly not to produce the happiness and fulfillment we seek. Perhaps we do this because we don't see any other possibility. What other choice do we have? Our thoughts seem so real and true, and they are very compelling.

Our thoughts are so prominent that we identify with them (we think that who our thoughts say we are is who we are), and doing that causes us to believe them. We really believe our thoughts are true, without questioning them. This is one reason we get into arguments with others: Others really believe their thoughts are true too, without questioning them. But where do thoughts come from? Are they really so trustworthy?

If you look, you see that your thoughts come from nowhere, and so do other people's thoughts. How can one person's thoughts be truer than another's when all thoughts arise from nowhere? If we didn't automatically accept our thoughts as true, we would soon discover how false most of them are and how contradictory they often are. We don't examine our thoughts because we are like a fish in water when it comes to them: Our thoughts are so much a part of us that we don't see them objectively. Not only do we accept them as true for us, but we also believe others should agree with what we think as well.

Thoughts are primarily conditioning, or programming, that comes from a number of known sources, such as family members, authorities, our culture, teachers, books, television, movies, the internet, peers, and friends. Conditioning also comes from more mysterious sources, such as experiences we don't even remember, including experiences we had in previous lifetimes. Our conditioning is made up of our particular beliefs, opinions, judgments, knowledge, and other ideas that are stored in our unconscious from all those experiences. Because everyone is influenced by different experiences, environments, histories, families, information, and teachers, everyone's conditioning is different.

Given this, it's difficult to imagine that anyone's thoughts are capable of providing reliable guidance for how to live. Our conditioning provides us with some useful general rules and values by which to live (it also provides us with a lot of useless facts, false information, and false values), but our conditioning doesn't help us make good choices in the moment. For this, we need something wise that can sort through the false, irrelevant, and contradictory information and beliefs that the mind uses to make decisions. For guidance that's specifically suited to the moment, we need something other than the mind.

What Guides Us

Our conditioning wouldn't be a problem if we weren't convinced that our thoughts are the right ones. Our conditioning would also be much less of a problem if our thoughts were true and helpful more often than they are. We expect them to be helpful because we assume they are true, but often, they lead us down the wrong path or confuse us with contradictory information. Our thoughts aren't meant to guide our lives, and yet we assume that is their role. The truth is that the mind is only useful for handling practical matters and mundane tasks, such as balancing a checkbook, following a recipe, using a computer, following directions, driving a car, reading a map, making plane reservations, and doing other mental tasks. The mind isn't wise enough to rely on for making decisions that shape our lives.

Something else is wise enough and *is* guiding our lives, Essence, but we often miss Essence's guidance because we are paying attention to our thoughts, to the egoic mind. Essence guides us in making choices, but its answers aren't always available when we want them. The ego wants answers now because it's uncomfortable with not knowing, even for a moment, so the egoic mind supplies answers, it decides something. The ego would rather make any decision than be in limbo, and often that is what the ego does. Essence, on the other hand, makes its guidance known in its own time and in its own way. To receive Essence's guidance, we have to be willing to wait and listen. But often the ego won't wait, and the egoic mind prevents us from listening by distracting us with endless chatter and analysis.

Essence allows us to be sidetracked by the egoic mind because that is part of the experience of being human. Essence is fine with having whatever experience we choose to have, based on the egoic mind's information and guidance. Essence tries to steer us toward happiness and our life purpose, and it usually does succeed, at least to some extent. So although our egoic mind shapes our life to a great extent, the egoic mind isn't the only thing shaping it. Essence has more power than we may think in influencing our decisions, despite the egoic mind's often heavy control.

As we evolve spiritually, the mind's control over us weakens and Essence becomes more prominent and apparent. When our choices begin coming more from Essence than from the ego, our experience of life often changes dramatically. The life that is created when the ego is prominent is often a very different one than the life that is created by Essence.

Essence's choices are often different than the ego's because Essence has different goals and intentions. Essence chooses love and unity over separation and superiority, it chooses peace and stillness over activity geared only toward getting more, it chooses service work over work that enhances the ego, it chooses meaningful work over work done solely for money, and it chooses a healthy lifestyle over an unhealthy one. And because Essence loves to create, creativity is often also part of Essence's activity in the world.

Love, peace, unity, service, meaning, creativity, and health are just some of the values Essence will organize your life around if you let it. On the other hand, the ego, while it may value these same things to some extent, values others things more highly and will choose those other things over Essence's values. The ego values money, prestige, security, fame, safety, power, success, beauty, comfort, and admiration. The ego puts these above other values unless those other values serve the ego's goals.

Those driven by the ego's values aren't happy. The ego's goal is to be superior to (and therefore separate from) others because the ego believes that superiority will ensure its survival and consequently its happiness. That is why the ego wants what it wants. However, achieving superiority, instead of bringing happiness, brings the opposite because happiness comes from love, and love isn't attained through superiority or by separating ourselves from others. Furthermore, our survival actually depends more on cooperation and unity with others than on competition.

When we feel our unity with life and with others, we feel love and we feel happy. This is really all any of us wants, but the ego works against this goal. The ego pretends to know what will make us happy, but it points us away from happiness. It drives us toward separation instead of toward love. Essence offers an alternative to the ego's drives and provides us with our only chance for true happiness by encouraging us to put love before selfishness and meaning and fulfillment before monetary gain. Essence entices us back to itself with glimpses of true happiness, peace, contentment, and love.

We do eventually discover the falseness of the ego and the trueness of Essence, but this can be, and usually is, a long journey, spanning many incarnations and millions of choices, all of which lead to learning of some kind.

What Spiritual Evolution Is All About

Life is certainly a mystery from the point of view of the ego. Life doesn't make sense—all the suffering and struggle, and then you die. To the ego, life is a struggle to survive and get to the top of the heap and stay there. Although the body can't escape death, the ego acts as if there is no end to life. The ego certainly feels there shouldn't be. If the ego had its way, it would get everything it wanted, including immortality.

To the ego, success is satisfaction of its desires. Being able to make life comply with its desires is the ego's strongest desire and its biggest fantasy. The ego doesn't seem to notice that life only occasionally conforms to our desires, even when we do everything that's supposed to get us what we want. But that doesn't stop the ego from desiring or from pursuing its desires. Desires structure most people's lives because most people listen to their thoughts and act on their desires, most of which come from the ego.

Although the mind is sometimes used by Essence, the mind is primarily used by the ego. So if you are listening to your thoughts and acting on them, you are probably allowing the ego to guide your life instead of Essence. Here are some questions that will help you see the truth about your mind and about your true nature:

Exercise: Looking at the Mind

What is this mind that has so much power to rule us and structure our lives? Why do we listen to it and believe what it says? Why do we mistake ourselves for the mind, when we are clearly more than that? What, after all, is it that is aware of the mind? What is this awareness, or consciousness, that observes everything, even thoughts? Who is this observer, this awareness? Is it even a who, or is it something vaster? Does this awareness have a location or a boundary?

These questions can help you realize your true nature, for you are not the mind, your thoughts, your beliefs, your desires, or your feelings. You have thoughts, desires, and feelings — they come and go within your body-mind — but who you are is what is aware of this activity and so much more.

When our awareness is focused on the mind, however, our thoughts seem to be more important than they really are. Our awareness contracts around thoughts and identifies with them in a way that makes them seem real and believable. When our awareness is redirected away from thoughts to something else, like sensations, then our awareness becomes identified with sensations, which then seem more real and important than they are. Wherever our awareness lands, it identifies with that. Given this, it can be difficult to recognize that our true self *is* this awareness (which is why the true self is often called *Awareness*), because this awareness is always involved in something and rarely experienced as separate from what it is aware of.

The process of spiritual awakening, or realization of our true self, is a process of becoming aware of ourselves as Awareness. The course of spiritual evolution is a gradual dis-identification with the false self, or the ego, and that which flows from it—thoughts, beliefs, opinions, judgments, desires, feelings, memories, hopes, fears, and fantasies—and a reunification with the spiritual self, or Essence, what we truly are, which is devoid of those mental constructs.

We are all evolving toward pure Awareness, which is not identified with the body, mind, desires, or feelings but knows itself as All. Until we have achieved this level of dis-identification, we are identified to some extent with our body, mind, desires, and feelings. Those who are deeply and more completely identified with these things suffer greatly, and those who are less deeply and completely identified with them suffer less. So spiritual evolution takes us from nearly complete identification and suffering to occasional identification and suffering to no identification and no suffering. Everyone is somewhere along this course. Here are two simple questions that will help you experience Essence:

Exercise: Experiencing Essence

Everyone knows what dis-identification from the false self, or ego, feels like because everyone has at least brief glimpses of it, even daily. Essence, your true self, is never apart from you, and it is most easily experienced by simply becoming aware that you are aware: What are you aware of now? What is it that is aware? Just asking those two simple questions will drop you immediately into the experience of Essence.

The kinds of experiences that most cause us to become aware of Essence are those that quiet or stop the mind: moments of beauty, moments of awe, moments of surprise, moments of emergency, moments of pleasure, moments of intense focus, and moments of deep relaxation. Anything that interrupts our tendency to pay attention to the flow of thoughts from the egoic mind or helps us become absorbed in something other than our thoughts, such as meditation, a hobby, a sport, dance, music, art, or some other creative activity, is helpful to our spiritual growth, because interrupting the domination of the mind, however briefly, allows us to experience Essence.

The more we experience Essence, the more we want to experience it. The desire to experience Essence is what moves us along on the spiritual path. Being involved with Essence is more rewarding than being involved with the egoic mind. As a result, we learn to align with Essence and detach from the egoic mind because we see that the egoic mind is the cause of our suffering, and we no longer want to suffer. Until then, we believe the egoic mind has the answer to our problems and to our suffering. It claims to, and we believe it.

Once we have experienced Essence enough, we come to see that there is another way to live that isn't focused on thoughts and driven by desires. Rather, a life lived aligned with Essence is a spontaneous expression of our true nature in each moment. Who knows what we will say or do next? Not even Essence has that planned out. Life is lived in response to what is flowing out of the moment. Each moment has the key to what we will do or say next, and what we will do and say isn't thought about, planned, or known ahead of time.

As you can imagine, living from Essence is a very different way of living. And yet many moments of your day are lived this way already, so this way of being isn't unfamiliar. As you begin to live more from Essence, life becomes simpler. Life isn't necessarily easier, however, since the same challenges exist, but our attitude and approach to those challenges doesn't turn life's difficulties into a problem. Challenges seem more stimulating and interesting than problematic, although they still require our energy and attention.

The ego is what labels anything it doesn't like or desire as a problem, when the only problem really is that the ego doesn't like or desire that. Essence doesn't have a problem with anything that's happening because it doesn't have a judgment, opinion, desire, or story about it. Judgments, opinions, desires, and stories are the spin the ego gives to experience, which causes the ego to resist life and consequently to suffer. To Essence, every experience is valuable and appreciated because, for Essence, experience is the purpose of life.

What Happens When Desires No Longer Fuel Action

Desire may seem like the bad guy because desires are behind much of our suffering. However, desire and free will are integral to evolution. The free will to follow our desires allows the Divine to have a variety of experiences, which is the Divine's intention. If we didn't desire, we wouldn't act, and action brings about experience and learning. It's no mistake that we have desires. The Divine intends that we have desires for as long as we are alive. They are as much a part of being human as having a body. Desires come into the mind and are fueled by feelings and acted on, and our life unfolds accordingly. This is as it is meant to be.

A time comes in our evolution when our relationship to our desires changes, however. At some point, many spiritual seekers experience a dropping away of their desires, which often results in a period of non-action, until Essence more clearly takes hold in that body-mind and moves the person as it chooses. This transition period may be almost nonexistent, or it may last years. This period can be confusing and upsetting to those who find themselves without the usual motivation. They may feel betrayed by the spiritual path, as they feel left without any clear direction. Although this lack of motivation and direction disappears with time, this experience can be very disconcerting not only to those experiencing it, but also to those dependent on or intimately involved with those experiencing it.

This period of non-action and uncertainty is often necessary to break the bond with the egoic mind. During this time, what used to be fun to think about may no longer be interesting or compelling. We may try to go back to thinking as we used to, but thinking seems hollow and unreal. We are too aware of the falseness of the false self, and we can't buy into it anymore. The experience may be one of boredom, emptiness, or sadness, as we mourn the loss of the old self and the loss of the excitement we got from desiring, dreaming, fantasizing, and making ourselves special through judgments and other stories we told about ourselves and others. We realize that the self we *thought* we were isn't real, so we can't get interested in creating a story about that self, any more than we are interested in that self's previous stories. There can be a feeling of "What now?" or "So what," as we are left with nothing to drive us in the world and no sense of our old self.

Of course, Essence does have intentions for us, and it will eventually make its intensions known to us. Meanwhile, things are changing energetically within us, which will manifest in the future as an ability to live in Essence and express Essence more consistently. During this confusing time, we shouldn't assume that nothing is being accomplished just because we may not be as busy acting in the world as we have been. A great deal is happening internally, in subtle ways, that is preparing us for future action on the part of Essence as it lives through us.

The old self has died, and it can take a while before the new Self is ready to express itself through our body-mind more fully. The death of the old self can be so slow that it isn't really perceptible while that death is happening, the only evidence of it being sadness and grief. Only later, will it become apparent that a death and rebirth has occurred.

Those who don't have insight into what they are going through may feel like they are a bit crazy and out of step with others, and they may judge themselves accordingly. Any judgments only make the process of transformation more difficult. A new negative identity may form around the fact that we are no longer motivated to do the things we used to do. We may see that as a problem and see ourselves as troubled, lazy, depressed, or having lost our spiritual connection. The ego often defines this spiritual process of disintegration of the old identity in negative ways such as these.

The ego is still alive and well during this process, and it will spin new stories and try to create new identities to replace the old ones. Those stories need to be seen for what they are: lies and partial truths made up by the ego to create a problem for the ego to solve. The ego wants something to do, and if it can't get us to act in the ways it was able to before, it will try to find other reasons for us to take action in its behalf.

So the ego paints this transitional period as a problem and tries to provide a solution. It tries to stir up feelings so that it can feel its own existence again. Without desires and feelings and the ability to move us with them, the ego has little reality. The ego is nothing without thoughts, desires, and feelings, so it will continue to try to create, or recreate, itself through thought by spawning problems and feelings.

Those who have some understanding of the spiritual process they are going through will see through the ego's ploys, but those who don't have this understanding may become entrapped in a new identity of themselves as someone who is lost, lazy, troubled, depressed, or confused. Those who have gone through a similar transition can be a voice of assurance for anyone who is experiencing such a disorienting time. Spiritual teachers and counselors often serve this role, but they may have to have had this experience themselves before they can be of help.

Two Kinds of Desire

Desires are stronger on some days than on others, but there probably isn't a day that goes by for anyone that desires don't arise. Where do they come from? If we knew the answer to that, we might see desires differently. As it stands, we generally accept desires as meaningful and true for us, whatever they may be. This is an assumption that isn't necessarily true, however.

Desires are part of our programming. We are programmed to have certain experiences in this lifetime, and desires help bring about those experiences: If you are programmed to experience wealth, you will have a desire for wealth. If you are programmed for spiritual progress, you will have a desire for that. If you are programmed for a particular lesson in relationships, you will desire a relationship with someone who will provide that lesson. What one person desires may be what another person doesn't desire. So desires vary greatly from person to person, depending on our programming.

That programming is determined in part by the astrological chart, and it can be uncovered by studying the chart. The astrology signs represent drives, which manifest as desires. These desires are meaningful when followed because they bring about the experiences we are meant to have. They unfold our life in the way it is meant to be unfolded. Desires that stem from the astrology chart are related to the intentions that the Divine has for our life. They come from Essence.

There are other kinds of desires, however, that are less meaningful because they don't contribute to the life purpose or the life lessons, as the drives in the astrology chart do, although these other kinds of desires do bring about experience and growth in their own way. These desires belong to the ego, and they are desires for things that make the ego feel superior and safer in the world. Examples of desires that arise from the ego are the desire for power, admiration, success, an impressive car, large amounts of money, fame, beauty, and expensive possessions. Those are things every ego wants, so these desires are universal, although they are stronger in some people than in others.

The desires that come from the astrology chart are sometimes in conflict with the ego's desires. For instance, the chart may drive someone to pursue a career that isn't particularly lucrative, although it is fulfilling. People who respond to the desires that come from Essence, as reflected in the astrology chart, are much happier than those who respond to the ego's desires. This explains why it's possible to be very happy while having little power, recognition, security, beauty, fame, or money. If getting the things the ego wants were necessary for happiness, then those who don't have those things would never be happy, and that simply isn't true. In fact, some of the unhappiest people on this planet are the beautiful, the rich, the powerful, and the famous, because beauty, riches, power, and fame alone are not enough to make us happy.

Contact with Essence and expressing it in the world is what makes us most happy. When we are responding positively to the drives in our astrology chart, we are expressing Essence, and that feels good, regardless of what that expression looks like. For example, a janitor can be supremely happy if service work is what he or she is programmed for astrologically, especially if that person performs the work well. The same is true of any role or task: If it fits our chart and we are expressing the drive positively, we will find fulfillment in doing so. Contact with Essence feels good, and that good feeling reinforces the behavior.

Contact (or identification) with the ego, on the other hand, doesn't feel good. Even if we achieve the ego's goals, feeling more powerful, beautiful, famous, or rich than others doesn't actually feel good, at least not for long, because feeling better than others separates us from them, and separation is painful. What we really want and what really makes us happy is love, which is a state of non-separation, of experiencing our unity with another or with others. Contact with Essence is the experience of love and unity, while contact with the ego is the experience of separation. Happiness can't be found in activities that only serve the ego because serving the ego is not necessarily serving the Whole. We belong to Oneness, and that Oneness is fulfilled by service to broader goals than the ego's.

Living with Desire

It isn't easy to live so closely with our desires. They drive us, consume our energy, and cause us to long and pine for things that currently aren't present. It's painful to want something we don't have, and that is exactly what desire is: It is wanting what isn't presently here. If what you wanted were here right now, you wouldn't need to desire it. Inherent in desiring is a feeling of lack, of something missing. Also inherent in desire is the feeling, or belief, that if whatever we wanted weren't lacking, we would be happy.

We long for what we don't have because we believe that having it will finally bring us peace and happiness. We don't realize that the lack of peace and happiness we are feeling is actually a result of desiring what we don't have. The desire is the *cause* of our unhappiness, not the fact that the desire is unfulfilled.

When we examine desire more closely, the truth about it becomes obvious. Desire is painful. We suffer because we believe we are lacking something necessary for our happiness. That's a very sad (and untrue!) story, but that story is essentially everyone's story. Everyone feels this way because the mind is programmed to be unhappy with whatever is happening. No matter what is happening, the mind comes up with complaints about it or ways to improve on it. That is the ego's job. That's what it is programmed to do, and it does that job very well. The ego refuses to be happy because if it didn't come up with reasons to be unhappy, it would be out of a job, since the ego is in the business of problem-creation and problem-solving.

This situation is painful for two reasons: It's painful to not have what we want, but it's also painful to discover that there's no end to wanting, even after we do get what we want. What we really want is the peace that comes from no longer wanting. We hope to experience peace and happiness once and for all by getting what we want. However, peace and happiness aren't achieved by *getting* but by loving whatever is showing up right now, just the way it is. We are so afraid that if we love life just the way it is showing up right now that we will never get what we want, when loving whatever is showing up *now* in our life has been the secret to being happy all along!

Loving whatever is would seem to be the simplest thing possible to do. Loving whatever is involves no effort, no struggle, no longing, and no disappointment. But loving what is showing up right now goes against our programming, so doing so is difficult. It requires vigilance to counteract the egoic mind's automatic rejection and resistance to whatever is happening. To experience the peace and happiness that exist in the present moment, we have to stop listening to the egoic mind, which undermines that peace and happiness with complaints, judgments, and fantasies of something better. These are the tactics the ego uses to take us out of the present moment and into the ego's world of desires, hopes, and dreams. The ego woos us with fantasies of a more perfect world, a more perfect mate, a more perfect experience, and a more perfect *me*, all of which are unreal and will never be real.

No matter how much we fantasize about the future, our fantasies will never come close to what will be, even if they are realistic (which they usually aren't). Have you ever imagined the future and had it turn out exactly as you imagined? So if thoughts can't predict or create the future, then what is the point of fantasizing? That's a good question and not one the ego is anxious to ask or try to answer. That question pierces through to the truth: Our fantasies, dreams, and desires don't create reality or even reflect reality accurately, although they do affect our experience of reality. When we are focused on our desires, dreams, and fantasies, we are not experiencing the present moment, and we are missing out on the richness, peace, and happiness that are right here, right now.

CHAPTER 2

Dreams, Fantasies, and Other Illusions That Drive Desires

The Nature of Dreams

We dream of our desires being fulfilled. We spend a great deal of time imagining how we want life to be. We imagine, ponder ("What would that be like?"), and plan. We imagine how we will feel when we get what we want, and then the suffering begins, as we come back to the reality that the dream is only a dream. The only way we can justify dreaming is to believe it's possible to achieve our dreams, but is it really? It's not that people never achieve their dreams, but the reality never looks or feels like the dream. So much is left out of the dream—all the usual problems and negatives that are part of reality. Unlike our dreams, reality is a mixed bag of things we like and things we don't like.

Dreams only include the positive. This one-sidedness is what distinguishes a dream from reality. Because the nature of reality is duality, reality has both aspects we like and dislike: Swimming pools are great fun, but they are expensive, and someone has to clean them. Rolls Royce cars are beautiful, but they still need their oil changed, and what if they get dented? There isn't a thing you can own or an experience you can have that doesn't have a flip side to it, including the obvious fact that things get old and experiences end.

Only in our dreams are we able to hold on to what we want and not experience what we don't want. That's why we like our dreams. At best, our dreams give us a break from the harshness of reality. At worst, they make it difficult to cope with that harshness. Our dreams have a place, but exactly what is that place if, in fact, our dreams don't actually create reality nor accurately reflect it?

Most of us assume that our dreams are meant to be fulfilled. We believe they are meaningful and have a purpose. Our dreams spur us to action, but is the goal—the dream—a worthy one? We assume it is, or why would we have that dream? Like every other thought, we assume our dreams are true. We believe in them, and they define us to some extent: "I am someone who wants...." We see others who want the same things as comrades, and those who don't want the same things as different or strange. Our dreams shape our choices and actions. They shape our lives.

The problem with assuming that our dreams are meaningful and that achieving them will make us happy is that dreams and the desires that drive them are just thoughts, most of which come from the ego, which isn't so wise about what will make us happy. We assume our dreams are our personal prescription for happiness, and that just isn't so.

Some desires come from a deeper place, from Essence, and they do have the potential for bringing fulfillment and happiness. Essence generates desires, urges, and images to inspire us to move in a fulfilling direction. These desires, urges, and images often become food for the ego, which builds fantasies around them. These fantasies aren't real, and they aren't particularly helpful. They can even hinder the achievement of Essence's goals. Like every other fantasy, these fantasies will never match the reality that Essence is trying to bring about.

A funny thing happens as part of the dream-creation the ego is engaged in: The ego creates a dream, and then it stirs up a fear of never attaining it. Although it's true that reality will never match our dream, the ego's message is that it's our fault if it doesn't. The fear that we may not get what we want, which we believe we need to be happy, fuels our desire to have what we are dreaming of and involves us deeply and personally in that dream: We fantasize about it, long for it, feel bad about not having it, and make plans and take steps to get it.

The ego makes getting our dream not only about being happy, but also about succeeding as a person and having a successful life. Personal fulfillment becomes linked with a specific dream. We feel we have to have our dream fulfilled to be good enough, to be a success, to have a good life, to be happy and at peace, to fulfill our destiny. Identifying with the dream this way makes the dream really important. Getting our dream becomes a test of our value as a human being and of the value of our life. What began as a simple fantasy becomes something we have to have to be happy and have our life work out. This is how the ego creates suffering.

Dreams that come from the ego are just not that important. It's an illusion that they are meaningful. Just because we have a dream doesn't mean it is meant to be fulfilled. The ego's dreams are part of our programming as humans and not meaningful messages from "on high." All egos dream of similar things. Many of our dreams are from the ego, but the ego is hardly a worthy guide for how to live our lives.

Take, for example, the dream house. Nearly everyone has an image of a dream house. Does that mean you will have or should have that house someday, either by working for it or through some other means? That's often the assumption, but that assumption isn't true. The image of our dream house doesn't predict our future house, nor is it necessarily an assignment to carry out. Many dreams we have are just thoughts that the ego gives meaning to with more thoughts. Thoughts generate feelings that motivate us to try to create that dream, and sometimes we are able to create something that approximates it. There is nothing wrong with following such dreams and creating what we are able to. The point is that the creation of something starts with a thought that often has no intrinsic meaning or truth, although we assume it has meaning or we give it meaning.

This doesn't mean there are no true dreams that do have meaning for us; however, these truer dreams don't come in the form of *specific* images. Essence releases impulses to create something in the world, like a dream house, but the specifics of how it will look aren't given to us ahead of time by Essence, or even known. Any specific image you have of a dream house or of anything else you dream of is generated by the ego, as it attempts to foretell and affect what will happen. The mind doesn't like uncertainty, so it makes up a complete image and pretends that's how it will be, or should be. That image may not match what Essence intends or would create, but that image has the potential for shaping what happens, and Essence allows that—or it may not. Thus, when a dream manifests, it is usually a co-creation between the ego and Essence.

If Essence is co-creating your dream house with you, you will be inspired with ideas about it in the moment. The dream house (or any other dream) unfolds organically, moment by moment, as each step in the creation process makes itself known in its own time. Sometimes you are flooded with ideas about what you are creating; other times, they trickle in as needed. And those ideas may change as new information is assimilated. The creation of anything is a process that unfolds over time. The timing and manner of that unfolding isn't under our control and can't be anticipated, and it doesn't happen in response to a static image held in our mind.

Although many believe that holding an idea of something in their mind long enough and strongly enough will cause that thing to manifest, this simply isn't true. Many other forces besides our thoughts are at work in creation, especially Essence's intentions for us. If this belief were true, then many more people would have what they wanted and imagined. Even when we do get what we want, it never looks exactly like we imagined. It's impossible for anyone to imagine something exactly as it will be, and yet many people feel like failures because they haven't been able to manifest what they have imagined.

The mind comes to some very irrational conclusions at times, and the idea that we can get what we want just by holding the thought of it in our mind is one of them. Nevertheless, the ego clings to this belief because the ego wants this to be true, because if it were, that would give the ego some sense of control in a world where the ego, in fact, has very little. Instead of delivering the desired result, this strategy of trying to think a dream into reality produces suffering because it is ineffective, and people tend to blame themselves when it fails. However, if these individuals looked around, they would see that no one else is succeeding with this strategy, except the few whose dreams happened to be exactly what Essence intended them to have anyway. Getting what we dream is more likely the result of having tuned into what was already meant to be than having "manifested" it with our minds. Even so, such individuals had to make it happen with their own actions, not just their thoughts. But the ego doesn't encourage such a rational approach because it doesn't want the falseness of this cherished belief exposed.

The ego wants us to believe it can get us what we want. It wants us to believe it's a worthy and trustworthy ally so that we will continue to turn to it. If we didn't believe in the ego's ability to guide and assist us, the ego would be out of a job, and it wants to exist in its current capacity, even though it fails miserably at bringing us happiness.

The flip side of this issue is that if Essence wants a particular dream fulfilled, it will be fulfilled when Essence wants it fulfilled, whether we imagine it or not, as long as we follow Essence as it drives us in co-creating that dream.

The Truth About Fantasies

A fantasy is a dream that has the details filled in by the mind. A fantasy starts out as just a thought. As more thoughts and feelings become attached to the initial thought, that thought turns into a desire, which is the thought and feeling "I want." A story or stories are added to those thoughts and feelings, and a dream is born. Feelings and stories make the dream feel very real and important. They give it a dimensionality that thought alone doesn't have. When specific details are added to this dream by the mind, we have a fantasy. Those details make the dream seem even more real.

The more detailed the fantasy, the more real it seems. And the more real the fantasy seems, the more we want it to happen, and the more we believe it will happen. This process is easy to see in others, such as some contestants on the TV show "American Idol" who are convinced that their dream is within reach just because they've invested so much emotional and mental energy in fantasizing about it. Because their fantasy seems so real to them, they assume their dream will come true someday. A sense of destiny develops around their dream that can't be argued with. They are convinced that they are destined to have what they've been imagining, regardless of any evidence to the contrary or whether they've actually done what is necessary to achieve it.

Fantasies are dangerous. They have the potential to create a lot of suffering because they put a demand and expectation on life that will never be fulfilled. All fantasizing is doomed to failure and therefore destined to cause suffering. The amount of suffering caused by a fantasy is in direct proportion to the amount of time, belief, and emotional energy invested in it. The more we believe a fantasy, the more we suffer. There's no exception because fantasies aren't true, and when we invest in something that isn't true, we will be disappointed. Investing in a fantasy is like investing in a gold mine that doesn't exist: We wind up empty-handed and unhappy.

The trouble is we love our fantasies. They give us pleasure because we believe them. But that pleasure is fleeting because we can only believe our fantasies as long as reality doesn't contradict them. As soon as we stop thinking, the fantasy disappears, and it's replaced with reality. No one can sustain a fantasy for very long, so we have to ask ourselves: Is fantasizing really worth it?

The reason that fantasizing seems worthwhile is because we believe it has some value beyond the pleasure it gives us and the relief it offers from what we perceive as a negative reality. Fantasies hook us not only because they are pleasurable and offer an escape from reality, but also because we really believe we are able to predict, control, and create the future by thinking about the future. That belief keeps us tied to our fantasies even when they stop giving us pleasure.

The mind goes back again and again to a fantasy, not only to get pleasure from it, but also to try to get some resolution from it. Fantasizing leaves us with a sense of incompletion. It makes us feel as if something is missing in our life and that our life won't be complete until our fantasy comes true. As a result, the present seems like a time of waiting until our dream is achieved. We feel discontent with life as it is. Life feels less than it can be and less than it should be.

An unfulfilled desire or fantasy not only leaves us feeling incomplete, it is also bothersome and annoying. Like an itch that needs scratching, we feel consumed with doing something about what we desire. Consequently, every fantasy generates many others thoughts that are about how to get that dream to come true. The mind becomes very busy with that problem in hopes of putting an end to the sense of incompletion and the torture of desiring. Unfortunately, the mind isn't actually very good at figuring out how to make our dreams come true because it's out of its league. The mind just isn't powerful enough to get reality to go its way, although it pretends to be.

Having a fantasy is actually more painful than it is pleasurable because the pleasure lasts only momentarily, while the pain of not having what we want can interfere with experiencing and appreciating what we do have in the present moment. It's sad indeed to miss the present moment because of a fantasy, especially when that fantasy floods the moment with the pain of incompletion, frustration, worry, fear, anger, and sadness. Those are the real fruits of fantasizing.

Fantasy not only takes us out of the moment, which is

actually full of everything we need and are looking for to be happy, but also fosters a secondary, or false, reality that results in painful thoughts and emotions. Fantasizing may seem pleasurable, fun, and harmless, but the short-lived pleasure and fun actually come at a high price. Nevertheless, we don't usually blame our pain on fantasizing but on the fact that our fantasies are unfulfilled. So we keep going back to our fantasies instead of this rich, present moment, which is so free of pain and full of peace.

The Truth About Reality

What's so bad about the present moment that we keep choosing a dream of something else over it? Is the present moment really so bad? The mind often thinks so. It often complains about and judges whatever is happening. Desires, by definition, are for something other than what is here, right now. Because the ego's job is to create desires, the ego has to find the moment undesirable. The ego is designed to reject the moment, no matter what is happening, so the ego comes up with reasons for rejecting whatever is happening or with ideas for how things could be better.

The ego is designed to try to change and reshape every moment, while the ego has little power to actually change reality. The ego tries to affect the way things are by thinking: It imagines that something should be different and what that would be like if it were different. But all this thinking doesn't change reality, only our experience of the moment. The ego causes us to be discontent with the present, with however life is showing up. When we feel discontent, it is a sign we are identified with the ego because discontentment is the ongoing experience of the ego. The ego creates and maintains discontentment. That is its job and what it was designed to do.

Why would the Divine design something that causes suffering? This is the million-dollar question. The ego is the antagonist in the drama of life. Without an antagonist, the drama wouldn't be a drama. There would be no story, no challenge, and no hero. This story is really about the hero, the one who finds his or her way back to the Divine, the one who is waking up out of the ego. Without being lost in the illusion of separation and without the challenge presented by the ego, there would be nothing for the hero to overcome. A hero is someone who overcomes challenges by developing ingenuity, strength, love, wisdom, and other positive attributes with the help of allies, including the gods.

The hero's story is the story of good overcoming evil. In our story, evil is played by the ego, which was programmed by the Divine to play that role. Within us, we have both what is capable of thwarting us and thwarting goodness and what is capable of supporting and saving life. Which will win out? Eventually, goodness does. In the meantime, the egoic mind is a formidable opponent because we are programmed to believe it.

We believe the egoic mind until we see the truth about it. It isn't worthy of our allegiance and it isn't the voice of truth or integrity, but the opposite. We learn this in part by discovering that there is another voice that is truer, wiser, and worthy of our allegiance. We come to know this truer voice over time, as it becomes stronger. Before that, the voice of the egoic mind is loud and strong and convincing. Nevertheless, following the ego's voice doesn't deliver the happiness it promises. Eventually, we become disillusioned with this false voice, and we begin to see that there's another possibility, another way to live, a truer voice to follow.

It takes many lifetimes to discover that truer voice and to

develop the inner strength, wisdom, love, patience, fortitude, and commitment necessary to break free from the domination of the egoic mind. Time and time again, our commitment is tested, and we must choose Essence over the ego until choosing Essence becomes automatic and natural. Eventually, the programming that keeps us identified with the ego becomes so weak that the egoic mind becomes quite powerless over us, and we only occasionally find ourselves involved and identified with it, and then only briefly.

It is not only possible to be free of the domination of the egoic mind, it is also our destiny. How long that takes is largely a matter of commitment. What are you choosing in this moment? And in this one? The more often you choose to identify with Essence's qualities, such as love, peace, and acceptance, instead of the egoic mind, the sooner you will become free. Essence allows us to identify with the egoic mind and to suffer as long as we wish. There's no judgment about how long awakening takes. Essence isn't in a hurry. Essence has all of eternity. Some people evolve slowly and some evolve more quickly. It's up to each of us to choose what we will give our attention to in every moment: love or fear.

This statement flies in the face of those who say that there is no choice and there is no one to choose because everything is One. And so it is. But the experience within the body-mind in this reality is that choosing happens. Whenever we identify with the egoic mind rather than just *experience* the present moment, we have made a choice to identify, although often an unconscious one. So we might as well become aware of having chosen that and then choose more consciously and end our suffering. Knowing that everything is One doesn't change the experience in duality—in *this* reality—where choosing can't help but happen, and where choosing, in fact, is integral to evolving out of duality.

This world of duality may seem like a harsh reality. There's so much suffering here. It's difficult to understand why the Divine would actually choose to create such experiences for itself, and yet it does. Our inability to understand this mystery is not the measure of its truth or a measure of the value of this experience in duality. We aren't capable of fully understanding the nature of reality, where it is going, or how the Divine is benefiting from it. Our minds can't comprehend the Intelligence behind all that is, which includes such a juxtaposition of good and evil, of suffering and bliss. We are humbled in the face of such immensity and mystery. It is as it is.

What Is Real

What we can know is the present moment. We can't know the future or the workings of the universe, but we can know what's true now in the present moment. Is happiness here, right now? Is peace? Contentment? Love? Acceptance? All of those feeling states can be felt in the moment because they are the real experience of the divinity within you, of Essence. What is more real than any thought, desire, fantasy, or dream is what is present now in the stillness in between your thoughts, desires, fantasies, and dreams.

What exists in this space? Awareness exists: awareness of the present moment and of all that the moment contains, including thoughts. The Awareness that we are is aware of and accepting of everything, but Awareness's reality is the experience of love, peace, acceptance, contentment, and oneness with all of creation. Its reality is not one of separation, discontentment, judgment, and desiring. It loves what *is* with all its Heart. It even loves the suffering, the illusion, the falseness, and the confusion. The ego runs from the pain and confusion, but the Divine embraces every experience because every experience and everything is an expression of itself.

The Real, the Divine, Essence, Awareness—what we really are, which goes by many names—can only be experienced in the present moment because there is no other moment. The egoic mind, on the other hand, is focused on other moments, on moments in the past and future, which don't exist. The ego's reality is a false one, a mental one. What makes its reality false is that it's too narrow a reality. Thoughts, dreams, desires, memories, fantasies, and emotions do exist, but they are a small part of reality, and they portray reality according to the ego. The reality of the ego is a distorted one that reflects its perceptions, conditioning, and agenda.

When we are focused on the egoic mind and the fantasies, desires, and feelings it generates, we can't be focused on other aspects of reality. We can only give our attention to one thing at a time. If we give our attention to our thoughts, we will miss out on whatever else is present. This wouldn't be a problem if thoughts from the egoic mind were true and valuable, but most aren't worthy of our attention. What is Real, on the other hand, is worthy of our attention because what we get in return is happiness, peace, contentment, and love. What we get when we give our attention to the egoic mind is the opposite: discontentment, dissatisfaction, and unhappiness.

We are fascinated by the egoic mind and the opinions, beliefs, fantasies, desires, and feelings it produces. In addition to believing the mind, we find it interesting and entertaining. It offers analysis, information, viewpoints, and judgments about everything. It's like having the TV or radio on continuously. What's playing in the egoic mind doesn't matter as long as something is playing. Almost anything will do to entertain us. It doesn't even have to be true. In fact, the more sensational and outrageous it is, the more fascinated we are by it.

When we turn to the egoic mind, we aren't just looking for information and guidance. We are looking for entertainment, and we are endlessly entertained by our opinions and judgments. They serve to set us apart from others and make us feel superior, but they also entertain us. We love gossip columns and opinionated personalities for the same reason: They entertain us because they stimulate our own opinions, which we enjoy immensely.

We love our opinions, judgments, desires, and beliefs. We also love trips down memory lane, and we certainly love our dreams and fantasies. We love these because we are programmed to love them. And we are programmed to love them because if we didn't, we would lose the sense of *me* that they provide. What would we be without them? Who would we be? Who *are* you without your opinions, judgments, desires, beliefs, memories, dreams, and fantasies? What's left? Nothing. Exactly.

We don't really like to be confronted with the possibility that we are nothing, that who we *think* we are doesn't really exist and that it isn't who we really are. We would rather have our opinions, judgments, desires, beliefs, memories, dreams, and fantasies, even though they cause us to suffer, than be without them because without them we experience that we are no-thing. Being nothing is a real problem for the ego. The ego is all about being somebody, which is the opposite of being nothing. The ego is in the business of denying the truth about who we are and creating a false you. That *you* is rarely happy, but at least it exists.

But of course, the real you exists. That is all that exists. The real you just can't be identified and defined by the mind, so it seems like nothing. The false you—the ego—is the *you* that doesn't exist. It pretends to exist, but it only exists as a mental construct, a thought about who you are: "I am...." The real you can't be defined in words such as these. Words are too limited to contain or express it. The real you is too big for the mind to understand, so the mind concludes that there is nothing else here.

The fact that the mind can't grasp the truth of who we are isn't really a problem because who we really are knows who we really are. To realize this too, all we have to do is stop paying attention to our thoughts and notice what's aware and conscious. It turns out that the real you has been here and aware of who you are all along. The egoic mind has just been overshadowing and obscuring the truth. Once we see this, the egoic mind isn't a problem. We know we are not the egoic mind but what is aware of the mind and everything else. We are Awareness.

The truth is that simple. The mind causes so much confusion, so many misunderstandings about life, but the truth is actually very plain and simple. It's staring us right in the face or, rather, it's staring right through our eyes, and it always has been. You are that Awareness rather than any definition of yourself you have ever held. Once we see this, we begin to recognize that that Awareness is who everyone else is as well. The Awareness that we are is the same Awareness that everyone else is too! What a mystery this is at the base of all life. And yet it's very plain and obvious once we begin to question the egoic mind and its assumptions.

Desires and Dreams Are Not Meaningful

The belief that our desires and dreams are meaningful is a core assumption, which we rarely question. We can't become free from the domination of the egoic mind without questioning that assumption, because desires and dreams are key thoughts that keep us tied to the egoic mind and busy with plans for getting what we want. Dreams and desires also generate a majority of our feelings: When our desires and dreams are getting met, we are happy and confident; when they aren't, we are unhappy, sad, angry, ashamed, and fearful.

We don't like not getting what we want because not getting what we want results in feelings we don't like. In particular, not getting what we want often makes us feel powerless and afraid. We feel that if our desires and dreams are meaningful, we should be able to attain them. If we aren't able to attain them, we feel we've failed at something important. We feel as if our life is going wrong. Or worse: We're afraid we will never have the life we want and that that will mean we are doomed to unhappiness, failure, and shame.

We take our desires and dreams very personally. The assumption that our desires and dreams are meaningful implies that they are *personally* meaningful, that they are specially made for us. If we aren't able to attain what we want (preferably immediately), we may feel ashamed, as if we failed at a mission we were given. We may feel betrayed by life and by ourselves. We thought we were powerful enough to make life happen our way, and now we see we aren't. That's a blow to the ego, which assumes it is that powerful.

This revelation is humbling, which is a good thing because this discovery points to the truth: We aren't the one in control of our destiny. We co-create alongside something else that is shaping our life. The ego pretends that it is the shaper of our destiny, but like most pretenders, it's eventually found out. When that happens, unless we are able to accept that our desire or dream may not have been a worthy one, we may feel very bad about ourselves.

It can take many experiences of our dreams failing before we begin to catch on that maybe our dreams are not true or meaningful. Maybe other things are more important than our dreams. Maybe the dashing of our dreams and what is learned from that experience is more valuable than the fulfillment of any dream.

Having our dreams dashed forces us to see that life goes on, and it goes on as it always has: unpredictably and beyond our control. Having dreams and desires gives us a storyline, a sense of destiny, while life is never that clear. We don't really know where our lives are going, but having desires and dreams gives us a script, so we think we know: The plan is to fulfill our desires. This plan, however, was created by the ego, and the ego doesn't really know what life intends for us. It doesn't know Essence's plan or even that there is a plan beyond its desires. The ego is convinced that its desires and dreams are what life is all about, and we believe it.

Having desires and dreams gives the ego something to do. It gives our life structure. What will I do today? I'll go after what I want. End of story. No need for further questioning. Desires also keep us focused in the mental realm, where plans are made for getting what we want and fantasies are created that drive those plans forward. All this mental activity keeps our attention off of the deeper questions about life and gives us a pseudo reason for being. It would be one thing if following the ego's desires brought us happiness, but the ego's lack of success at making life turn out the way it wants and its shallow values eventually cause us to question the value of our desires. If life isn't about desire-fulfillment, then what is it about?

The ego has no answer to this question, but Essence does. Essence's answer, however, doesn't come in words. Its answer is released in the moment, as Essence moves us forward toward more meaningful activities, ones that don't necessarily fulfill the ego's desires and dreams but fulfill us on deeper levels. The trouble with being focused on desire-fulfillment is that pursuing our desires can take us away from more meaningful activities. Our attention and energy is either going to be taken up by the egoic mind or by the spontaneous movement of life that is Essence. Fortunately, even when we are largely caught up in desire-fulfillment, Essence moves us toward its goals as it is able to through our intuition, in between all the thoughts. Essence can still reach us when we are caught up in our thoughts, but it could reach us much more easily if we didn't believe the ego's plan was a worthy one.

Eventually, we do come to see the uselessness of the ego's drives and guidance, and we begin to express Essence more and the ego less. We come to see the ego's desires and dreams for what they are: just thoughts generated by the egoic mind that have little bearing on our happiness or on the meaning of our lives.

Fear Is Not What It Seems

We are afraid of fear and feel it is a very bad sign because we believe our fears and think they mean something. We think that our fears have the power to foretell the future. We relate to desires and fears in the same way: We trust our desires and our fears and give them the power to shape our choices.

Desires and fears come from the same place (the ego), and

both are illusions with no intrinsic meaning. They are therefore poor guides for what to do in life. They are just conditioning. Desires and fears go hand-in-hand: Fear holds desires in place and drives them. Fear convinces us that our desires are important. No other thought is as effective in driving us toward what we desire as the fear of what might happen if we don't get what we want. Many of the things we want, we want because we believe that they have the power to prevent what we fear. For instance, we want to be beautiful (in the case of a woman) or rich (in the case of a man) because we are afraid we won't be loved if we aren't. We fear not having our desires met because we believe we need them met to be safe and happy. This just isn't true.

Getting what we want doesn't make us safe or happy because safety and happiness aren't obtained through our efforts. Rather, safety and happiness are subjective states—inner experiences. When we are identified with the ego, we experience a lack of safety and happiness; when we drop into Essence, we experience safety and happiness. Happiness, peace, contentment, and safety—everything we truly desire—are subjective *experiences,* which already exist within us and aren't achieved through effort. We already experience these subjective states, but the ego creates the opposite experience by telling us we need something to be safe or happy or at peace. If we believe the ego, it will keep us busy trying to find happiness and safety outside of ourselves, when happiness and safety were never missing in the first place.

Our fears are unfounded. Every fear is nothing but a negative thought about the future. It neither has the power to create nor the power to predict the future. Our fears don't even have survival value. If anything, they interfere with our survival rather than protect us. But we are all meant to learn this, and seeing this is part of our evolution. Fear is one more illusion spun by the ego to keep the desire-game and the ego's illusory world going.

Fear keeps us in the ego's clutches, identified with the ego instead of with Essence. Fear scares us, and scary thoughts are difficult to ignore. When a fear arises, it gets our attention because we believe it provides information we need to survive. Furthermore, the ego convinces us that it has the solution to what we fear, so we stay involved with the ego and with the thoughts it produces about what we are afraid of.

Fear also makes the ego's reality more real. When fear is tied to a thought, that thought seems very real, because fear is not only an emotion, it also produces a physical reaction within the body, and what could be more real than that? Have you ever been so convinced that a fearful thought was true, even though it wasn't, that your body reacted to it exactly as if it were? Our imagination can make something seem so real that it convinces our body. Fear is that powerful, but only that powerful.

Fear is actually impotent, although it makes *us* feel impotent. Our fears only have power if we believe them. If you never believed another of your fears again, you would be just fine. The reason our fears have power is we believe they keep us safe. This belief is difficult to see through because it's so deeply ingrained: We are afraid to not believe our fears. We are afraid that if we ignore our fears, they will come to pass. This fear is totally irrational, and it's good to see that it is irrational. That's how we become free of the programming. In seeing the truth about our fears, they lose their power to scare us or move us in any other way, and then we are free to see what's really true.

What is true and real reveals itself only in the present moment, not in a thought about the present moment or in a thought about the future. Fears are always about the future, and as such, they have no value for the present moment. If something potentially dangerous is happening, fear, which results in panic, isn't a useful response. If we don't allow ourselves to follow our thoughts at such a time, which are likely to be fearful and negative, we will find ourselves responding naturally and spontaneously to whatever is happening. That natural response, which comes from Essence, is free from fear and free from thoughts about what is happening.

When we simply respond to life without thinking, then any experience, no matter how potentially frightening that experience is, is just an experience that requires a response. We suffer because we tell ourselves stories about what we are experiencing while it is occurring (and afterwards), and these stories scare and upset us: "This is terrible. This shouldn't be happening. I can't handle this." These stories aren't helpful or true because they don't and can't represent the whole experience, which is much more complex than any story you could tell about it. Many people in the most dire of circumstances recount having what feels like a spiritual experience because the intensity of the situation they were in caused them to be very present, without their mind interfering. Any experience you are fully present to is not only bearable, but can be almost mystical, as it is infused with the power of Essence.

One of our strongest desires is for survival. The ego is concerned with our survival, and it uses fear to try to help us survive. It scares us away from dangerous things, and there's some value in that. Knowing that fire burns and cars can kill is useful, but the ego isn't much use for deciding what to do in specific situations. The ego parrots the knowledge and rules that are stored in the mind, but the ego doesn't know how to apply them. The wisdom of how and when to apply our knowledge only comes from Essence.

When we act wisely, we are acting from Essence, not from the mind. The mind does provide useful information at times, but information isn't really what we need in a dangerous or critical situation. We need action that's informed by wisdom, and that action often takes place in a split-second, without thought. In critical situations, there's no time to think, analyze, and evaluate, which is what the mind does best. In a crisis, what saves us is responding from Essence instantly, without thought. The most effective actions are those that arise when the mind is quiet. When danger is present, the mind is actually a liability. In those instances, basic safety rules are of no use.

Memories Don't Make Us Happy

Like every other illusion, pleasant memories can't make us happy. Going over a fond memory for pleasure is like trying to eat a picture of a cookie instead of the real thing. A picture of a cookie can't satisfy because it isn't real. A memory is a poor substitute for reality. Nevertheless, we often try to revive memories of a time when we got what we wanted. When we feel something is missing in our current reality, we often try to get from the past what we feel is currently missing by remembering a time when that wasn't missing.

When we really let ourselves experience how empty and unsatisfactory our memories are, we find that dwelling on our memories, even of a great experience, is more frustrating than it is rewarding. Still, we are convinced that if we could just stay with a memory long enough or focus on it hard enough it would eventually satisfy us. We try to get back that good feeling we once felt and make it stay, but we can't. As soon as we stop focusing on the memory, it and any feelings attached to that memory disappear instantly. We can't hold onto a memory because we aren't able to concentrate on it for more than a few minutes. Other thoughts, images, and feelings creep in, phones ring, and reality intrudes in other ways. We don't have as much control over our memories as we would like. For many reasons, the experience of a memory doesn't come close to the actual experience.

Our memories are missing so many details. Memories are spotty and often highly inaccurate representations of the past. However, we often don't care how accurate our memories are because what we really want from them is happiness, pleasure, fun, love, and our desires fulfilled. We turn to our memories because we hope that they will make us feel good. As a result, memories often get distorted by our imagination. We embellish them, either intentionally or unknowingly, because we prefer a more perfect reality than the one that actually existed or the one we recall.

Even the past isn't good enough for the ego, which is always wanting to change reality. Only a more perfect memory will do. Unfortunately, even an embellished memory can't satisfy us. If only our memories and fantasies did satisfy us, then we would be grateful to our ego for bringing us so much happiness. Instead, our memories and fantasies leave us feeling empty, and they make it even harder to be happy with reality as it is. Our pleasant memories, like our fantasies, create discontentment, not happiness.

Reality isn't actually bad, but the ego's job is to make reality seem that way. The ego focuses on what it doesn't like, not on what it does like, so it is always discontent. There are things that are enjoyable and pleasant about any moment, even from the ego's standpoint. But the ego doesn't focus on these things because its job is to create discontentment and problems, which give the ego something to do, a reason for being, or what would we need the ego for? To exist, the ego needs to be needed. Without the problems it creates, it would have no purpose. Its job is to think up solutions to whatever it defines as a problem.

The ego creates problems by defining something as bad or undesirable and then supporting that judgment with reasons. The ego doesn't give reasons for why something is good, only bad. In leaving out half of the story, the ego skews our perception so that we see only the negative side of something. The reason we believe the ego's spin on things is that its voice is an opinion we tend to want to agree with because we identify its voice as our own, so we more readily take on our own ego's perspective than someone else's. We naturally jump on our own ego's bandwagon. It feels right to agree with our own thoughts. Furthermore, our ego's opinion doesn't feel as much like an opinion as *the truth*. We want our ego's opinions to be right because, after all, they are *our* opinions. Even when those opinions and beliefs create suffering and problems, we believe them because we often don't see an alternative.

Most people automatically accept the opinions, beliefs, judgments, and other thoughts that arise in their mind as theirs, and they assume these thoughts are true. Most people aren't able to separate themselves from what they think. Realizing that our thoughts don't belong to us and don't represent who we really are is a huge step in our spiritual evolution. That realization frees us to discover that there's something else to identify with besides the egoic mind. Until then, it seems like the egoic mind is who we are, and we have only brief glimpses of Essence, which we may not recognize as our real self. Once we start questioning the egoic mind, we begin to see that something else is living our life.

CHAPTER 3

Working with Desires

Freedom from Desire

Not everyone wants to be free from desire, and for many, that's appropriate. There is a place and a reason for desire, or it wouldn't exist. Desires create experiences, and the Divine wants experiences, even painful ones. Desire makes the wheels of life go around. Desire is what drives life, as well as being the cause of suffering. Nearly every activity we engage in is driven by some desire: We cook because we want to eat, we study because we want a job, we dress nicely because we want love and admiration.

Although challenging, desire is an integral part of life. With greater awareness, however, our relationship to desire can entail less suffering. Although we will never be free of having desires, we can be free from the need to have our desires met. We suffer not because we have desires, but because we feel we have to have them met. It is possible to have desires but not suffer over them. We suffer over them because we believe that getting them met is essential to our happiness. That misunderstanding is what leads to suffering.

For most, the solution to the suffering that desire causes is to try to get what is desired. Consequently, many spend their lives going after what they want, which is what they believe will make them happy. But there is another solution to the suffering caused by desiring what you don't have, and that is to see desire for what it is: Desire is just the thought "I want...." Can a thought cause suffering? Yes, if you agree with it. Who or what is this *I* that wants?

When you see that the *I* is the ego and not who you really are, the experience of wanting is put in perspective. Wanting is forever coming out of the ego. If you give your attention to wanting what you don't have, you will be chasing one desire after another. The ego is in the business of manufacturing desires. There is no real rhyme or reason to what the ego desires. It wants one thing and then another. Often, the ego wants opposite things (e.g., "I want a relationship, and I want to be independent"). The ego wants whatever it thinks of or whatever it sees. It's easy to see the ego at work in small children in stores: "I want that. I want that. I want that!" People are designed to want. Wanting is automatic and not meaningful.

Once we are able to separate ourselves from the *I* and see how undiscriminating, random, and constant the ego's wanting is, we gain some distance from our desires, and there is freedom in that. We can be more objective about our desires. They no longer seem like they belong to us, and that makes them less compelling. What makes the "I want" so compelling is that the "I want" is happening inside of our own head. So we identify with that voice and believe we do want what the *I* wants and that we need what the *I* wants to be happy.

Once we have some distance from the *I,* we can choose to listen to what the *I* wants or not. We are more able to evaluate the desire and come to a conclusion about it ourselves when we have some detachment from the thoughts in our mind. Sometimes desires are worth listening to, or at least harmless. The desire for some ice cream, for instance, or for some other pleasure can bring enjoyment if it isn't indulged in too often.

Desires have a place, but it's important they stay in their place and not take over, which is what tends to happen. The more we are identified with the *I*, the less likely we are to be discriminating about our desires, and the more likely we are to indulge them without questioning them. Indulgence is an easy pattern to fall into, especially with physical desires. The more we say yes to them, the more they tend to arise. So physical desires in particular require objectivity and discrimination. The ego isn't able to be objective about a desire because it generated the desire. But something else is able to be objective, and that is Essence.

Essence is wise about desires. It knows which desires have value and which don't. And it knows how much to indulge a desire before too high a price is paid. From Essence, we are able to relate to our desires in a balanced way, without either depriving or indulging ourselves. When it comes to desires, let Essence choose which ones to pursue and which ones to ignore.

Exercise: Examining "I Want"

Notice when the thought "I want" arises. What does that thought arise around most often? What does the I want most often? Is it really true that you want that, or is that a desire that arises habitually? What will getting what you want mean? What are the other ramifications? The ego assumes that getting what we want will be all positive, but getting what we want always has a number of ramifications, some of which aren't so positive.

Once you have some objectivity in relation to a desire, you can choose whether to pursue or indulge that desire or not. When you see the whole truth about what you think you want, you may decide you don't want it after all. Not all our desires are worthy of our attention and energy. Something other than the mind is needed to determine what's of value to us and what isn't. Is your desire aligned with Essence?

The Desire for Physical Pleasure

As humans, we have a desire for physical pleasure, which serves our survival to some extent. The desire for sex and food are the most compelling pleasure-related desires and potentially the most problematic. Other such desires include the desire to be touched, the desire for beauty, and the desire for comfort. Everyone has these desires. They are natural and serve a purpose in maintaining life and bringing enjoyment to life.

The pleasures that derive from the body and senses are meant to be enjoyed. They are purposely designed by the Divine, which enjoys life through us in these various ways. However, when any of these pleasures is taken too far, the opposite happens: pain and discomfort. This is how these drives are kept in check. For example, we can only eat and have sex so much before it becomes painful and impossible to continue.

The ego will drive us toward pleasure until it turns into pain because the ego doesn't have the wisdom to temper this drive. Pleasure is one of the ego's strongest values, and the ego often chooses pleasure over health and even wealth and other things it desires. Pleasure is basic to the ego, and the drive for pleasure is primitive and irrational. The ego doesn't consider the consequences of pursuing its pleasures. It only imagines the rewards. But like everything in this world of duality, the pursuit of pleasure has a down side: Overindulgence has a price, and pleasure-seeking may take the place of more meaningful activities. Pleasure is only so satisfying, and that satisfaction doesn't last.

The ego is driven toward gratification, and the sooner it gets it, the better, or so it thinks. It has difficulty delaying gratification for a more long-term reward. It would rather have an insignificant and fleeting reward now than a more meaningful, long-lasting one later. The ego isn't rational. It is impulsive and wants pleasure now, no matter what the cost later. This is easy to see in the realm of food. The ego grabs whatever it wants and gobbles it down. When we become more aware of that impulsiveness as it is occurring, we begin to have some choice around it.

Because eating is such a basic need and a great pleasure, the ego often takes over this activity. Table manners were designed to help balance the ego's tendency to wolf down food. Noticing the urge to gobble down food is an important step in gaining some objectivity and control over this behavior. When you feel that intense drive to wolf down food, it means you are identified with the ego. Once you realize this, it's possible to switch your identification to Essence by simply becoming aware of what your senses are experiencing while you are eating.

When the ego is relating to food, it isn't really connected to the sensory experience of eating and tasting. The ego is driven by impulse, and when we are identified with it, we go unconscious and don't really take in the full sensory experience of eating. However, when we drop into the sensory experience, we drop into Essence, and Essence knows how to get full enjoyment out of the experience. When we are fully involved in the sensory experience of eating, there is more satisfaction from what we are eating and less need to continue eating past the point of satiation.

The same is true of sex: The more aware we are of the actual sensations during sex rather than our thoughts about the sensations or about something else, the more satisfying the experience is. When the ego has sex, it is driven to completion, and it misses the moment-to-moment experience. Essence, on the other hand, relishes the journey and takes its time. It is present to the actual sensory experience and not to thoughts. The main difference between the way the ego eats or has sex and the way Essence does is that Essence isn't trying to get to the end of the experience. The ego is focused on the endpoint, and Essence is focused on the moment-to-moment sensory experience.

This difference is key in staying balanced in relationship to food and sex. When the journey is satisfying, as it is when we are identified with Essence, there's less need to repeat the experience. When we are identified with the ego, on the other hand, we feel like we never have enough because we missed the experience. How can something you weren't really present to satisfy? It can't. When we become more present to what we are doing, then whatever we are doing becomes more pleasurable and satisfying.

Another difference between the ego and Essence is that when we do come to the end of some pleasure, Essence is grateful, while the ego is discontent. Consciously choosing gratitude over discontentment at this point moves us into identification with Essence and releases us from the endless cycle of wanting. When we are identified with the ego, even when our body has had enough of some pleasure, like food, we may still feel we want more just because the egoic mind convinces us that we do. The thought "I want" isn't true or meaningful, but we assume that it is, so we may indulge in more of something even when our body doesn't want more. When that's happening, it's important to pay attention to your body instead of your mind. The mind will push for more pleasure, no matter how satiated you feel, but the body knows the truth about where pleasure ends and pain begins.

As real and as compelling as a desire feels, it is just a thought, and it will weaken and disappear if we don't give in to it. We master our desires by mastering our mind, which is a matter of learning to not identify with the voice in our head. We do this by becoming aware of the thoughts that are arising in the mind without doing anything in response to them. The key to not identifying with our thoughts is observing our thoughts as if they belonged to someone else. The more you can detach from your thoughts this way, the more mastery you will have over your desires, and the easier it will be to remain identified with Essence, which has a positive relationship to pleasure and other desires.

Exercise: Experiencing Pleasure

The next time you are engaged in a sensual pleasure, bring your attention fully to that experience. The ego has a tendency to rush through every experience and to think about the experience instead of be involved in it. To counteract that tendency, slow down and bring your attention to the sensations instead of any thoughts about the sensations or about the experience. Relax and let your body have the full experience without interruption from your mind. Everything is much more satisfying when it's fully experienced. This is true of even mundane experiences, such as doing housework, which can also be satisfying – and pleasurable.

The Desire for Comfort and Beauty

Comfort and beauty are basic to our quality of life. They align us with Essence because we relax and feel grateful when we are experiencing them. Relaxation and gratitude bring us into alignment with Essence because they are qualities of Essence.

Beauty is essential to our well-being. Beauty may not be the most basic need, since our survival doesn't depend on it, but our quality of life does. Fortunately, we don't have to possess beautiful things to experience beauty, since it is available to everyone through nature. The natural world is a gift from the Divine as well as an expression of the Divine. The beauty of nature inspires us, expands our consciousness, and brings us closer to our own essential nature. Through the natural world, we experience Essence, and that brings peace, happiness, and healing from the negativity of the egoic mind and its world. Through nature, we reconnect with who we really are, and that is a great gift.

Our natural drive for beauty and comfort can be taken over by the ego. When that happens, we suffer over wanting more beauty and comfort. The ego is never satisfied with what it has. To it, beauty and comfort are commodities it never has enough of. The ego doesn't notice or appreciate the beauty and comfort it has, only what it doesn't have. It feels it needs to own beautiful and comfortable things to be content, and that just isn't true. Beauty and comfort can be experienced in the simplest of ways: through a flower, the soft leaves underfoot, and the warmth and sparkle of the sunshine. Beauty and comfort are available for those who choose to notice them.

We can enjoy not only the beauty of nature, but also beautiful things that other people own. This includes physical beauty: We don't have to be beautiful to be happy. We can get as much enjoyment from appreciating other people's beauty. Once we experience our oneness with everything, even slightly, the separation between us and others lessens, and we rejoice in their beauty as much as we would our own.

Focusing on our own beauty only results in suffering and separation, not more love. It takes a lot of time, energy, and self-focus to look beautiful according to cultural standards, and such self-focus leaves us feeling empty. And ironically, instead of bringing us more love from others, being beautiful often inspires envy, jealousy, and lust. On the other hand, appreciating the inner and outer beauty of others activates our capacity to love and attracts love into our life. Such appreciation aligns us with Essence, and that makes our own inner beauty shine. Inner beauty is true beauty and attracts to us the kind of love we really want: true love. Love that comes from the ego is a poor substitute for true love because the ego's version of love is tainted with envy, lust, jealousy, and perpetual longing.

When we are identified with the ego and we see something of beauty, we want it for ourselves, we want more of it, and we are jealous of the possessor of it. This is pure suffering. On the other hand, when we are aligned with Essence and we see something of beauty, the Heart opens and we feel love. Noticing beauty can be a doorway into Essence instead of a doorway into the ego's hell of longing, lack, comparisons, and jealousy.

You can learn to relate to beauty from Essence by simply noticing when you are relating to beauty from the ego and then ignoring those thoughts and feelings. These thoughts and feelings belong to the ego, not to you, and you don't have to give them your attention. Choose to give your attention only to love. In turning away from the ego in this way, what is left is Essence and love.

Exercise: Experiencing Beauty

Notice the beauty around you. The gift that many artists give us is that they point out beauty that is easily overlooked by the ego, which surveys its surroundings with a critical, evaluative eye instead of embracing and loving what it sees for the simple reason that it exists. Essence loves all of existence just as it is. You can experience that love for existence as well if you allow yourself to drop out of the judgmental mind and into your senses.

The Desire for Love and Romance

Because love is primary not only to happiness, but also to survival, love is a strong drive and a strong desire within each of us. Essence drives us toward love, while the ego drives us away from it. The ego is conflicted about love because love is needed to survive, and yet, love runs counter to the ego's need to be separate and superior. "It's a dog eat dog world" is the ego's point of view. The ego tries to love because it needs love and because loving is expedient, not because the ego's nature is to love. With Essence, on the other hand, love flows naturally because Essence's nature is love.

Every desire is predicated on the absence of what we desire: We desire money, beauty, success, love, or anything else only because we feel we don't have enough of it. This sense of lack is the ego's usual state. It never feels it has enough of anything, including love. The ego desires love, while Essence *is* love. When we are aligned with Essence, there is no desiring, not for love or anything else. Essence is an experience of completion, not lack. Therefore, any desire for love comes from the ego, which has difficulty experiencing the love that is always present, underlying all life. The ego doesn't feel love (Essence does), so it doesn't feel *loved.* Any emptiness or lack of love we might feel is the ego's experience and has little to do with reality.

There is no shortage of love because love is at the core of all creation. However, the ego doesn't experience this love because wherever the ego looks, it sees lack rather than what *is* here. It doesn't notice the love that is present because it believes love is lacking. Our beliefs shape what we perceive about life. They filter our experience: If we believe love is lacking, we filter it out of our experience and experience only what we believe is there. Furthermore, life reflects back to the ego what it believes. So if we approach other people as if they are lacking in love, they are likely to respond accordingly. Others tend to respond to us as we are responding to them or according to the beliefs we are holding in the moment. Others commonly reflect back to us our inner state and thereby reinforce it and the underlying belief that created our inner state.

For example, when you smile, others are likely to smile back. The underlying belief that caused you to smile might be "Life is good" or "People like me" or "I like people." And when people smile back, that belief is reinforced. Or when you act annoyed, others act annoyed too. The underlying belief that caused your annoyance might be "People are so uncooperative" or "People are a pain" or "Life is a hassle." When people experience your annoyance, they feel annoyance too, which reinforces whatever belief you are holding. On the other hand, if we approach the world with love and a feeling of being loved, the world responds lovingly toward us. It mirrors back our loving state. So the ego creates both the sense of an inner lack of love and the actual experience of a lack of love as a result of its belief in and perception of lack.

A world that lacks love is the ego's reality and the ego's

experience, not Essence's. But we are here to discover love. Love is at the core of the great mystery in which we are participating. The truth seems to be quite the opposite at times, but the truth is eventually revealed to us. Before that, convincing the ego that love is behind all of life is difficult.

We long for love because we long for what is true and real. We long to return to our true nature, to Essence. Our longing for love is a longing for Home. So this desire actually serves Essence. Unlike other desires, the desire for love brings us to Essence. First we long for human love and romance (love between egos), and eventually we long for something truer and deeper: We long to experience the love that is at the depths of our being and everyone else's. Through human love, we have an opportunity to meet our divine nature in and through another. We see our own divine face in another's. Our relationships with others can be a meeting between our Essence and theirs, between our divinity and theirs, instead of a meeting of our egos. When that happens, it is a very pure form of love.

The longing to meet the Divine in another often gets translated into romantic illusions: We long for the ideal love, one who will love us perfectly, exactly as we are, and one whom we can love perfectly and easily. But this kind of love will never be as long as we remain identified with the ego. Egos interfere with love by blocking it with judgments, fears, beliefs—and fantasies. The fantasy of the perfect beloved is one of the greatest blocks to love because no one will ever live up to it. In the presence of this fantasy, even the most wonderful human being falls short.

Romance is a driving force in human evolution. It drives us to procreate, and it drives us to uncover the mysteries of love. The ego makes love difficult, and the journey toward love is one of overcoming the ego and discovering Essence. Romance is the juice and fuel that keeps us moving forward through all the disappointment, pain, and suffering of this journey. No one arrives at love except through pain. The pain comes from having to let go of judgments, fears, beliefs, and self-centered attitudes that keep us from being close to others.

Through our romantic relationships, we discover the falseness of our judgments and conditioning and the pain they cause others. At some point, if we want true love, we must choose love over our conditioning, over all the judgments that separate us from others and keep us from loving them. If we want to love, we have to master the ego by learning to detach from the egoic mind, and doing so can be a difficult and lengthy process. Choosing love may seem like an obvious choice, but to the ego, choosing love seems dangerous. It would rather have its judgments, superiority, and mistaken beliefs than love. So the ego isn't what ultimately chooses love. It is Essence that chooses love.

When you choose to love someone despite what you feel are his or her shortcomings, that is Essence, not the ego. The ego is strongly identified with whomever it loves and consequently doesn't tolerate shortcomings, which the ego sees as reflecting badly on it. When we are identified with the ego, our judgments, desires, expectations, and beliefs are more important to us than love. They define us, and we aren't willing to give them up, even for love. With Essence, it is different: Essence just loves. Essence accepts others with their flaws because Essence loves the human experience and all the imperfections of being human, and it rejoices in the uniqueness of each person. It celebrates the differences between people. Moreover, Essence loves because it recognizes itself in others.

Relationship is about recognizing our divinity in another, but the ego has different ideas about this. The ego enters into relationships for its own reasons. It is continually evaluating what the other person can and does do for it, and if that person comes up short, the ego withholds love. The ego loves conditionally and for selfish reasons. Therefore, its fantasies are primarily about need-fulfillment: The perfect person is someone who is what the ego wants him or her to be. People aren't valued for their uniqueness or differences, but for what they can do for the ego.

The desire for others to be different than what they are and to be what we want them to be is the source of pain in relationships. Since this sums up the ego's attitude toward relationship, then clearly, relationships between egos are doomed. True love is only possible from Essence, so if we want relationship and love, we have to learn to live more from Essence and less from the ego.

In relationships, the only legitimate desire is the desire for love. Other desires come from the ego and interfere with love by causing separation. So if we desire anything from a relationship or from another person, that desire will only interfere with getting what we really want: love. On the other hand, desiring love above all else aligns us with Essence, where we will find ourselves rejoicing in our differences and where we will find everything we really want: peace, acceptance, contentment, and love. What the ego wants isn't worth desiring because it takes us away from love. It's not a good choice. The better choice is love.

The Desire for Wealth, Fame, Success, and Power

Because the ego wants to be safe and secure, it desires worldly power, including wealth, fame, and success. This is the same reason the ego wants everything else it wants, including love.

The ego is primarily about survival, and it feels that being on top will ensure its survival and happiness. Survival is generally secured by getting things such as power, wealth, fame, and success, but often at a cost to happiness and love.

Happiness can't be found in power, wealth, fame, or success because the ego continues to be discontent even when those things are attained. The ego never has enough of anything, so if we listen to the ego, we will feel that we don't have enough, even when we do. Furthermore, when power, wealth, fame, or success becomes a driving force, little energy is left for more meaningful things that have a greater potential for bringing happiness.

There's a time in everyone's evolution for the pursuit of power, wealth, fame, and success for their own sake and for no other reason, and that time is usually in our earlier incarnations. These aren't particularly fulfilling lifetimes, but we learn important lessons from pursuing those things, so those choices are not a mistake. In our later incarnations, we are often talented enough to be successful doing what we love and what we find meaningful. The experience of power, wealth, fame, and success is quite different when these things are achieved as a result of pursuing something meaningful and intrinsic to our life purpose.

Something deeper than the ego drives us to develop our talents and pursue meaningful goals rather than the ego's more superficial ones. Everyone is driven toward something: learning something, developing a talent, serving others, creating, or expressing something. Whatever our life purpose is, we will be driven toward fulfilling it, and following that drive will be more fulfilling than pursuing power, wealth, fame, or success. The drive for power, wealth, fame, or success comes out of the ego, while the drives that truly fulfill us come out of Essence and are felt as pushes, urges, impulses, and inspiration.

Drives from Essence aren't propelled by fantasies, like the ego's desires are. However, sometimes the ego builds an elaborate story of fame, success, wealth, and power around a drive that comes from Essence. Fantasies such as these always belong to the ego because Essence has no need for fantasies. Essence enjoys the mystery around how its intentions will unfold. Not even Essence knows how what it intends will unfold or what that will look like. The ego, on the other hand, likes to pretend it knows because it doesn't like not knowing. It conjures up fantasies as a way of giving some shape to the unknown. It also hopes its fantasies will help manifest its dream. Even though the ego's fantasies are impotent, the ego would rather live in a pretend world, where it has what it wants, than in the real world, where what it wants isn't happening.

Grandiose fantasies are a sign of the ego. Essence encourages us to achieve its goals through inspiration, excitement, and feelings of happiness, not through fantasies. Fantasies imagine an unreal future, which doesn't serve the goal. Since reality will never match the fantasy, fantasies cause anger, discontentment, frustration, disillusionment, impatience, and disappointment more than they inspire. Although fantasies don't serve the goal, they do give the ego some relief from the constant state of wanting that it finds itself in.

Wanting so constantly and so strongly is exhausting. If we give a lot of attention to the ego's wanting, that wanting only increases, and so does our suffering. By giving the ego's wanting less attention, we can decrease our suffering. Then our attention is available for something more rewarding: the present moment, where true happiness, peace, wisdom, and contentment reside. When our attention is being given to the ego's wanting, then it isn't being given to something more fulfilling and true, something more real than our thoughts and desires. Shifting our attention from the ego's wanting to the present moment lessens our suffering and increases our peace and happiness. That's a good tradeoff!

The peace, joy, happiness, and contentment of Essence are right here, right now, but we may overlook these feeling states because we are paying attention to the loud and noisy mind and its demands: "I want!" Its demands get our attention not only because they are so loud in comparison to Essence, but also because they are so insistent and full of fear. The ego spins negative fantasies as well as positive ones. Every desire is tied to a story of doom and gloom. Permeating the ego's wanting is the fear of failure, death, loneliness, and unhappiness if it doesn't get what it wants. The ego tells a story that makes its desires feel urgent and important: "You may not survive, and you certainly won't be happy unless...." The fear that is stirred up by negative thoughts such as these fuels action, but having fear as a motivator is unpleasant.

Essence motivates us toward its goals with feelings of joy, elation, excitement, happiness, inspiration, expansion, and a sense of rightness or yes. These aren't thoughts, but feelings, or what might more aptly be called *positive feeling states*, to differentiate them from the feelings, or negative emotions, produced by the ego. Essence works more through the intuition and the body than through the mind, although sometimes Essence's ideas and inspiration do arise spontaneously in the mind, but when they do, they aren't preceded by thoughts.

Because the ego is a purely mental phenomenon, thoughts aren't as trustworthy as the deeper feelings that Essence communicates with. Those who are mentally focused most of the time often miss Essence's communications, which are not primarily mental. As we evolve, we become more willing and better able to hear Essence's subtle communications. The domination of the mind weakens, and we become more aware that more is going on than just thought.

This is an important step in our evolution because Essence can have only so much influence if we aren't tuned in to it. Once we become aware of Essence and how it communicates, it has a much better chance of getting through to us. And once we begin to let Essence lead us in our life instead of the egoic mind, our life can change quite dramatically. The ego leads us down a lot of painful and senseless roads.

The Desire to Be Free

Initially, the desire to be free can come from the ego because it wants to be free of suffering (which it has created). The ego doesn't know what it's wishing for, really, until it's too late. Being free of suffering requires becoming free from ego-domination, which certainly is not what the ego wants. But the ego has no choice: Evolution naturally proceeds from suffering to freedom, from the ego to Essence. The ego can't do anything about this. It is doomed. Everyone eventually wakes up out of ego identification. Thus, suffering is both the grist for our evolution and what eventually awakens us to our true nature. The ego is responsible for the very thing that causes its demise: suffering.

This means that as much as you might want to awaken, you also don't want to awaken. This is the dilemma of the spiritual seeker. Essence draws us toward itself, but the ego is only willing to go so far before it balks or becomes involved in subterfuge. The ego is willing to attend spiritual gatherings for its own reasons: to escape suffering, to improve its situation in life, and to gain spiritual power and knowledge. However, the ego finds reasons for not trusting the teachings or the teacher, it creates mental confusion, it stirs up fears, it criticizes and judges, it tells stories, and it denies the truth. All of the ego's thoughts, fears, doubts, and judgments are designed to keep us in our head instead of our Heart, where spiritual truth can be discovered. Once we drop into our Heart, the truth about who we are becomes obvious, and our thoughts quiet and our confusion disappears. But before then, the ego can put up a lot of resistance, even as it wears the garb of a spiritual seeker.

The ego sabotages spiritual progress because it sees that going in the direction that spiritual teachings point to will end badly for it. The ego can't withstand the scrutiny that spiritual inquiry brings to it. The truth is seen about the ego: It is not who you really are, and it has been lying to you all along. It has been pretending to be you and trying to run your life, but it isn't you and it isn't capable of running your life. And instead of making your life better, it has only made it worse. Once we really see this, we can't go back to believing the ego. Once we know that a lie is a lie, we can't believe it again. But it's still a long road to fully embodying Essence. The ego is seen through, but who are you really, and how do you live your life now?

It's not enough to see who we are *not*. We have to allow ourselves to fully feel, in every moment, who we really are and trust that to live our life. This means consciously turning our attention away from the egoic mind and toward Essence. Turning away from the mind takes diligence because we are so used to letting our thoughts guide our lives. We are so used to turning to the mind for guidance about what to do next. And the ego is happy to provide that, even though it doesn't know what is best. The ego makes up answers just to have them.

The answers to many of our questions about our life aren't

always available from Essence when we want them, but they are available when we *need* them! Before making a choice, we have to be willing to wait for a knowing about what to do, which will arise from Essence in its own time. The ego doesn't like not having answers, so having to wait for them is uncomfortable. The ego is in the habit of making a decision and taking action to ease the tension around not knowing. Any decision and any action relieves the discomfort of not knowing somewhat. Unfortunately, the decisions and actions that come from the ego may not be the best ones.

The hardest thing about letting Essence run your life is learning to wait for Essence's timing. We never know when we will be moved by Essence to do or say something until doing or saying happens. Essence doesn't let us know ahead of time what it intends and what it will inspire us to do. Essence's intentions don't show up in our mind as thoughts. Essence doesn't mull things over or make lists of pros and cons, like the mind does. So often, actions and speech that come from Essence are quite a surprise. You didn't know you were going to do or say that! But doing or saying that felt right, so you trusted that impulse or inspiration, although you may not know for quite some time if that impulse was right. Living in Essence is living in the unknown and learning to accept that.

Actually, we have always been living in the unknown, but we've been pretending to know because the egoic mind prefers that to not knowing. We don't know what is going to happen tomorrow or what we will do, but we pretend to. We decide to do something, and that makes us feel like we know what we will do, but we still don't know for certain if we will do that. How many times have you said you were going to do something and then suddenly done something else?

To be free, we have to fall in love with not knowing instead of being afraid of it. Embracing not knowing makes waiting and seeing what Essence has in store for us possible. When we embrace the unknown, it's such a relief. What a burden and struggle it is to try to know everything ahead of time, and what a relief it is to just admit the truth: "I don't know."

When our desire to be free or to awaken comes from Essence and that desire is very strong, we find we are willing to give up our other desires: the desire to know, the desire for control, the desire for spiritual knowledge and power, and even the desire to stop suffering. We surrender our other desires to the one desire that is left: the desire to be free, to be liberated from ego identification. You can't have your other desires *and* the desire to be free. Giving up your other desires doesn't mean you won't ever get what you want, though, because by losing your self (your ego), you gain everything. You see that, to be happy, you never needed what your ego wanted anyway. Once you see this, then giving up these desires is easy. If you are everything, is there anything you lack? When we are aligned with Essence, what we discover is we lack nothing, we need nothing, and yet, everything that is meaningful is given to us in full measure, including some of the things we desired.

Giving up your desires is nothing more than giving up a thought of wanting. Giving up your thoughts of wanting simply means not giving these thoughts your attention— ignoring them. They have never helped you be happier or even helped you get what you thought you wanted. Wanting isn't valuable, so giving up wanting is giving up nothing except for your suffering. Are you willing to give up your suffering? That's a question worth examining because, the truth is, the ego doesn't want you to give up your suffering, since the ego has no purpose without suffering.

We think that desires are so valuable. We think we will be

deprived if we give up our desires. But giving up our desires is like giving up a dream of cake for a real piece of cake. The fantasy can't compare to the Real, to the delicious present moment that is full of everything we really want and need.

CHAPTER 4

Creating Your Reality

Your Reality

When we are identified with the egoic mind, we live in the ego's world, and that becomes our reality. The more we detach ourselves from the ego's mental world, the more we taste reality, which is just what *is*, without all the mental images and stories that the mind overlays onto reality. Reality is whatever is actually showing up in the moment—what we experience through our five senses and also what we experience more subtly as intuition, internal drives, inspiration, and other communications from Essence.

The ego resists, rejects, and tries to change and manage reality. It does this rejecting and managing through thought. What it most tries to change and manage is the image of the *I* that we see ourselves as. The ego works very hard not only at giving the *I* some reality by dressing it up in all sorts of images, but also at making it the right image. This usually requires spinning a story about how the *I* is in relation to the world and to others. Many egos like to make the world and others wrong in order to puff up this image and make itself superior. Those who have a negative identity, on the other hand, have egoic minds that reinforce and support that negative self-image. This is accomplished by telling negative stories about life, the world, oneself, and others.

The egoic mind tells lots of stories. These stories create an inner world and perceptions about the outer world that are often quite divorced from reality. These stories don't include enough of reality but depict only a small part of reality. When we tell a story that reflects only a small part of reality (the part that reinforces our self-images and story), we are telling a partial truth, and partial truths are lies, by definition. People live in one false reality or another until they begin to gain some detachment from the egoic mind, which spins these lies.

Our reality is made up of the stories we tell ourselves the most. Some of these stories change over time, but most of us have core stories we cling to throughout our life (until we don't), which define us and give us a sense of identity: "I am someone who was abused. I am the golden child. I am inadequate. I am the princess. I am the loser. I am the different one. I am the one who can't do anything right. I am the reliable one. I am the adventurer. I am the clown. I am the martyr. I am the hard worker. I am the smart one. I am the caretaker. I am the risk-taker. I am the fearful one. I am the weak one. I am the skeptic. I am the loner. I am the victim. I am the leader. I am the rebel. I am the special one. I am the lazy one. I am the healer."

Core identities such as these take on a sense of reality and truth because they've been reinforced again and again by mental repetition that is either conscious or unconscious. Our core identities are also reinforced by parents, friends, and others we are close to, who pick up on our self-image and repeat it back to us. In most cases, our core identity was bestowed on us by a parent or someone close to us in childhood.

We all have a set of identities that are part of our overall self-image, which take on a life of their own because they are reinforced internally and externally. We begin to act in accordance with our various identities. For example, if you see yourself as clumsy and smart, you may trip a lot and study a lot. These identities are self-fulfilling prophecies: We make sure that life conforms to and agrees with our self-image by behaving in ways that cause others to agree with our self-image. And just to be sure, we tell others outright how we see ourselves and therefore how they should see us. We make sure others get our self-image right, just in case they didn't catch it in our behavior or demeanor. Here's an exercise that will help you uncover the beliefs that lie behind your self-images:

Exercise: Examining Your Self-Images

Take a moment to list some of the ways you see yourself. Do you notice any themes in the images you have of yourself? What underlying beliefs about yourself do these self-images point to? What do you believe about yourself?

Any belief you have doesn't have any truth or reality. Anything you believe about yourself is just a story you've been telling yourself, perhaps because someone significant in your childhood told you that about yourself. These beliefs are only true because you believe them. Take that statement in for a moment. Nothing you believe about yourself is inherently true. And yet believing what you believe about yourself has shaped your life and affected your experience of yourself, of life, and even of others. And what you believe about yourself has affected other people's perceptions of you. Beliefs are powerful if we believe them.

Having some insight into the reality created by the egoic mind and by our conditioning is important in breaking identification with the egoic mind and in learning to live from Essence. Unless you can see that you are not the self-images you are living out, it will be difficult to see who you really are, which has no image attached to it whatsoever. Who you really are can't be experienced as an image. It's too vast and too much like nothing to imagine it. The mind can't grasp who you really are, which is one reason it creates self-images that it can grasp. The mind overlooks the deeper reality behind life because it can't grasp it and, instead, creates a mental reality it *can* grasp and have some control over.

The inner reality and imaginations of the egoic mind spill out into outer reality largely through desires. These inner images stimulate desires, and desires stimulate activity. That activity structures our life: When we are ego identified, our life is based on getting certain desires met. Our particular desires are shaped in part by our self-images. For example, if you think of yourself as a princess, then you want what princesses want. Or if you think of yourself as a loser, you may either want to be a success or to be taken care of.

Many of our self-images cause us pain or a sense of lack, which we try to alleviate by getting more of something: love, money, beauty, success, education, or power, for instance. And if our self-image is grandiose, then we want to prove that specialness to the world. In any event, when we are identified with our self-images, our choices reflect those images, and desires fueled by those self-images create the impetus for many of our activities.

When we are identified with the ego, solutions to the pain caused by our self-images are offered by the ego. This would be fine if the ego were wise and had values that were worth pursuing, but the ego's values are opposed to the natural order of life, which is love and unity. Because the ego is all about separation and being better than others, its solutions are usually ones that attempt to achieve superiority rather than love.

When we are aligned with Essence, we don't try to overcome the pain caused by our negative beliefs and self-images by getting more of something or by trying to be better at something than someone else. Instead, we see that our self-images aren't real or true and that nothing is needed to improve or heal them. Our self-images are healed simply by seeing that they were never true and that the only power our self-images ever had was the power we gave them.

Our self-images just need to be seen for what they are. Then when all of our energy is no longer taken up by trying to fix this *me* that doesn't even exist, it's possible to discover what Essence wants from us in the present moment. How would Essence structure your life? What activities does Essence propel you toward? Those activities will always be more fulfilling than the ego's activities.

So *your* reality is just that: your own subjective reality. You create it with the stories you tell about yourself, your life, life in general, and other people. The egoic mind manufactures ideas about yourself, life, and others, and you see yourself, life, and others through the lens of these stories. They mediate between you and real life and shape your experience of life.

We don't create reality, which is a co-creation with many other forces, but we are responsible for creating some of the things we experience in life, and we certainly create our subjective experience of life.

Reality

Most people experience their stories more than they experience reality because they essentially live in a mental world and only occasionally come out of that world for a breath of real air. When they do, it can feel amazing. Reality is much richer and juicier than the egoic mind's ideas about it.

Reality is a very different experience than the subjective reality of the egoic mind. For one thing, reality isn't driven by desires, which are painful, but by love: the love of life, the love of growth, the love of discovery, the love of creating, the love of unity, and the love of love. Real life, without the ego's stories, is an experience of peace, unity, love, patience, compassion, and wisdom. This is the reality that everyone wants to experience, but the ego doesn't know how to experience that reality. In fact, the ego is what keeps us from experiencing reality and the peace, love, and joy inherent in it.

When we drop into Essence, into the moment, and experience reality, that experience is free of desire because desire is a thought manufactured by the ego that comes out of the ego's sense of lack. Egoic desires may arise when we are aligned with Essence, but we don't identify with them or take them as meaningful, so we don't go after them. They aren't something we want because we know the truth about them. We understand that desiring is just what egos do, and we understand that desire of this nature is the cause of suffering.

Reality is free of desire because reality doesn't need desire to unfold. Reality unfolds just fine without it. Something else is unfolding reality that isn't experienced as desire, but more like motivation and drive. In the ego's world, desire creates motivation, but in Essence's world, motivation just arises without a specified outcome.

Essence plays in life and is moved toward experience for many different reasons, usually to grow, serve, create, play, love, discover, express, and learn. Unlike the ego, Essence doesn't require a specific outcome to be motivated to engage in an activity. Any activity or experience can be a means for what Essence "desires": growth, discovery, love, creativity, learning, self-expression, and service. Essence is willing to play it by ear and see what an experience holds. Essence intends to use experiences for growth, discovery, learning, and developing certain talents and qualities, such as compassion, patience, and love, but Essence doesn't demand that life show up in a particular way.

The ego, on the other hand, wants life to be a certain way because it has specific ideas about what it wants and about what would be good or bad in regard to that. This attitude makes life a struggle. The ego doesn't know how to go with the flow of life. It's always trying to manage that flow, and that's exhausting. Trying to managing the flow is exhausting because the flow isn't easily managed. The ego has some impact on where the flow is going, but the ego is only one small player in the scheme of things.

The ego, fueled by its desires, is fairly impotent at achieving its desires. Reality has its own way of showing up and its own timing, and reality isn't particularly swayed by the ego's desires, plans, hopes, and dreams. The ego can make things happen only to the extent that other aspects of reality cooperate. Ultimately, reality has the final say, and sometimes it allows the ego's dreams to manifest, and sometimes it doesn't.

This inconsistency is very confusing to the ego, which believes it can or should be able to make what it wants happen. After all, at times the ego succeeds. Those successes are just enough to give the ego a sense of potency and to support this belief. The ego assumes that if it doesn't succeed this time, it will some other time. It's always looking for the magic formula that will get it what it wants every time. So the ego explores philosophies and esoteric and more ordinary means to uncover the secret to getting what it wants. You only have to look at the profusion of books about being successful and manifesting your dreams to see this in action. Many of them are bibles for how to get our way in life, for that's the ego's religion. Getting our way in life is what the ego worships, and desiring is how the ego worships.

For the ego to get its way in life, the ego has to be aligned with the Whole, with Oneness that is the truth of reality. When the ego is aligned with the Whole, the ego's desires manifest, not because the ego manifested them, but because the Whole allowed the ego's desires to manifest. The reason the ego's desires don't manifest more frequently is that its desires are often out of sync with the Whole and even at odds with it.

Oneness, or the Whole, has intentions. It operates as one Being. When the ego makes choices that support or at least don't interfere with these intentions, the ego gets its way. However, if the ego's choices interfere with these intentions, the ego won't get its way. The Being that we are knows what will assist and not assist the life it is unfolding. This Being allows egos to affect what it is creating, but it doesn't allow egos to rule over what it is creating. What would that be like, after all? Life would just be about getting what we want, which it isn't.

The Whole is teaching us to love, and it teaches this by showing us that selfish desires aren't worth pursuing. The Whole is wise, and it steers us in the direction of love by showing us the emptiness of the ego's values. We are here to learn to love, to discover our true nature. In the meantime, we experience ourselves as separate and driven by desires.

How to Tell If Your Desires Are Aligned with Essence

Some desires are worthy of our time and energy, and some desires aren't. Worthy desires are ones that potentially serve the Whole, while unworthy ones don't serve the Whole and may work against it. An example of an unworthy desire is the desire to have lots of money. There's nothing wrong with having lots of money or even with wanting lots of money. The problem is with wanting money at any cost, with making money the number one value. Greed is the name for this, and greed can be a very destructive force. When the desire for money or for anything else takes us away from Essence or causes us to harm others, that desire isn't worth pursuing.

The Whole allows us to play out our desires and experience the results of putting them first because that's how we learn that certain desires aren't worthy. The fact that greedy people often get lots of money may seem unfair, but getting lots of money is often what it takes to teach someone the emptiness of putting wealth above other things. Some desires are allowed to be fulfilled because they lead to learning and to different choices at some point. In these cases, life isn't rewarding ego-driven behavior, but teaching the limits of it. Because some lessons take many lifetimes to learn, a person's evolution in this regard isn't always obvious.

Eventually, we come to desire what Essence wants more than what the ego wants. But before then, we are run by the ego and its desires. As we evolve, what Essence wants becomes clearer, and what the ego wants becomes less compelling, so we naturally move toward Essence and away from the ego.

There's a very simple way to tell if your desires are aligned with Essence or with the ego: You can feel the difference. When we are pursuing desires that aren't aligned with Essence, we feel tense, driven, impatient, contracted, narrowly focused, and blind to the reactions of others around us. We see others only in terms of how they may help or hinder our goal. When we are aligned with Essence, on the other hand, we feel relaxed, joyful, motivated, in the flow, happy, fulfilled, and open and present to others and to the environment. Although the ego will try to co-opt our activity, and it may even succeed at times, when we are aligned with Essence, there's an overall sense of rightness and attunement in what we're doing. When we are aligned with Essence, we are sustained by that sense of rightness, while the ego is sustained in its pursuits by what it imagines achieving its goal will mean.

When the ego pursues a goal, it pushes ahead and uses the will to overcome obstacles. It relies on the mind to plan and strategize instead of on the intuition. If those who are ego-driven were to drop into their intuition, they would be dropping into Essence's territory, and they might not continue those pursuits, or continue them in the same way.

Essence's goals are carried out by following the intuition. The mind is used as needed for what minds are good at, but the mind isn't what orchestrates the activity. Instead, the activity arises naturally and spontaneously out of the moment. What will be done isn't planned or known ahead of time. Essence moves us toward its goals as it sees fit, and it brings us what we need to fulfill its intentions: people, information, opportunities, and emotional and financial support.

What the Whole wants from us is clear if we pay attention to something other than the egoic mind. To discover what Essence wants from us, we have to listen to the Heart, not to our thoughts. What the ego wants is apparent by paying attention to our thoughts, but Essence's drives and intentions aren't apparent through thought, but through joy, excitement, intuition, inspiration, drives, urges, and a deep sense of knowing. These things indicate worthy desires, and we will receive the support we need to fulfill these desires. Following our joy, excitement, intuition, inspiration, urges, and a sense of knowing will bring us fulfillment and happiness. However, Essence's intentions will be fulfilled in their own time and not necessarily when the ego wants them to be. The only thing that can interfere with fulfilling Essence's intentions is listening to our egoic mind or other people's minds.

We are often faced with the dilemma: Do I do what I *should* do or what is safe and secure, or do I follow my Heart? The answer is always to follow your Heart. But following our Heart isn't always easy. Following the Heart doesn't feel trustworthy to the ego, and we are used to trusting the mind to lead us. Furthermore, other people's egos are often giving us the same advice as our own ego: "Be careful. How will you pay the bills? You can't do that. You'll never make it." So even when what the Heart wants is obvious, we are challenged from within ourselves and from outside ourselves to follow the Heart's subtle counsel.

Because following the Heart can be challenging, many choose the safe course, the one they *should* take. The desires of the ego are so much clearer and louder than the unobtrusive voice of the Heart. Trusting that this subtle sense of what is right for you is actually what is right for you can be difficult and may take a lot of courage. And yet what is the alternative?

Exercise: Examining Where Your Desires Come From

What desires make your Heart soar? You can feel the intentions that Essence has for you. When you contemplate desires that come from Essence, you feel joy, not the giddy high of the ego's dreams, but an expansive, pure joy.

Make a list of your desires according to how they feel. Put the desires that make your Heart sing in one column and the others in another. Those in the other column may be desires that cause you to feel tense, worried, and stressed, as if not having these desires met will threaten your survival. Or those in that column may be things you imagine will make you happier. These are usually desires for more or better of something you already have: a new house, better clothes, a new car, and so on. Notice the different feeling quality between the two columns.

You are free to pursue desires in either column, but one column promises much more fulfillment than the other. Since you have limited energy and time, choosing well is important.

Co-creating with Essence

There are lots of reasons why things aren't the way we would like them to be, not the least of which is that this is just the way it is in this world. You aren't the only one not having the experience you would like! That's because this world isn't designed to please us. It's designed for many other purposes. This world provides the Divine with all kinds of experiences, not just pleasurable ones. Equally important, this world provides the Divine with an arena for creativity. When we are aligned with Essence, we love experience too and don't demand that it be pleasurable or to our liking. Experience is juicy, and difficult experiences are juicy and rich in opportunities for growth, creativity, learning, and transformation.

This world is an expression of the Divine's creativity, and we are both a reflection of that creativity and a potential force for further creativity. We are not static creations, but works in progress: We are continually being created, shaped, and honed by our experiences. Creation touches us, and we touch it. Every act of ours is a creative act because every act is totally original and unique. We will never again act exactly as we are acting now, and who knows what we will do next?

What we choose to do next may be a response to the egoic mind or to Essence (the Divine within us). Who knows? Whatever we do is fine with the Divine, which is having an adventure co-creating with us. The Divine designed us to be unique so that it could have a unique experience through us. When we are identified with the ego, the Divine has experience; when we are identified with Essence, the Divine also has experience. The Divine embraces all types of experience. Nevertheless, when we are aligned with Essence, the possibility exists to be more pure expressions of the Divine in the world. The Divine can use us directly to create in this world, which it created for itself to play in. We become the Divine's hands, legs, eyes, mouths, and ears. When we are able to step out of the way fully, life is very joyous.

Everyone is co-creating with the Divine to some extent. To the extent that we are doing that, we feel joyful and fulfilled, and to the extent that we aren't, we feel contracted and unhappy. What allows the Divine to express itself more fully through us is our willingness for expression and co-creation to happen and our ability to detach from and ignore the egoic mind, which has its own, very different, agenda. Only after much practice and commitment do we learn to detach from the mind.

When we are co-creating with the Divine, the mind isn't entirely out of the picture, of course. The mind is needed for the things the mind is good for. The difference is that Essence uses the mind instead of the ego. This is a very big step in our evolution—when the mind is no longer dominated by and under the control of the ego. Then Essence can use the mind in a way that is highly creative and productive. Inventions, innovations, and new ideas that revolutionize old ways of doing things or old ways of thinking enter the world through the minds of those who have turned them over to Essence. Art, music, and every beautiful thing—whatever makes our spirits soar—come through minds such as these.

Some of those who bring such creative expressions through are still identified with the ego much of the time, but they are able to allow the mind to be used by Essence. This is one way the Divine creates through us. It uses our mind to create. When the mind is used in that way, creative inspiration arrives in the mind, but not through thinking. Those who produce in this way often have no idea of what they will create—creating just happens. They feel that what they've created just came through them, and they can't really take credit for it.

The ego would like to have this type of creative experience, and it tries to, but the egoic mind only interferes with this type of creativity. There is a vast difference between creations produced by the egoic mind and its conditioning, and creations brought *through* the mind by Essence. When we experience Essence's creations, they align us with Essence. Egoic creations, on the other hand, often express conditioning, although even they can serve in reflecting more relative truths. But when absolute Truth comes through a mind, we are touched deeply. The power of some art and other creations comes from the fact that they align us with our own true nature, and that's a powerful experience, especially for those who aren't used to experiencing that.

The ego creates as well. It explores life through its own lens, and it enjoys and learns from that. Even when someone is creating from the ego, Essence is involved to some extent. Essence involves itself in every activity as much as it is allowed to be involved. In any moment, we can align with Essence or with the ego. It's our choice. Most people's lives are a co-creation between the ego and Essence, as they move back and forth between the two. Essence allows us to create from the ego, and it offers its input and suggestions intuitively while that is going on, which we are free to notice and include or not. Whatever we are creating will be more fulfilling the more Essence's input is included.

The ego's desires can interfere with Essence's creative process. For instance, maybe you have artistic talents that Essence would develop in you, but your conditioning or self-image drives you to want to do something different. Maybe you think you should be a business person instead of an artist. You want (or think you want) to be a business person because you like the idea of that and the security of that, and you ignore your desire to be an artist because you don't like your ideas about what that would be like. If you pursue business, that will make it difficult for Essence to create through you in the way it intended, but Essence will do its best to express those talents within the life that you create. However, if you let Essence design your life, that will be more fulfilling for you. Essence is willing for you to have the experience you choose, but some choices will be more fulfilling for you than others. Choosing what Essence wants for you rather than what the ego wants will always be the more fulfilling choice.

When we are identified with the ego, we may make choices that create a life that is different from what Essence intended for us. And when we try, within the structure we created, to be happy, we may not succeed. The way Essence steers us toward happiness and fulfillment is often through unhappiness or difficulty. If we are living a life that isn't meant for us, we won't feel happy. To move us out of our life structures, Essence might create difficulties or roadblocks, or it might catapult us out of those structures some way. Sometimes Essence deconstructs our life in order to reconstruct it. In that case, Essence will bring us what we need to reshape our life, but we still have to be open to Essence's intentions for us. Times of crisis open us up, whether we want that to happen or not.

Getting What You Want

The Rolling Stones expressed a great truth about life when they sang: "You can't always get what you want—but you get what you need!" To be happy, we have to learn to love getting what we need rather than what we want, when getting what we want isn't in the cards. Being happy when we aren't getting what we want requires trusting Oneness, trusting that life brings us what we need, if not what we want. The ego doesn't trust Oneness, of course, because the mind can't comprehend Oneness. This is why the ego doesn't trust life. Besides, trusting Oneness and trusting life puts the ego out of a job. The ego sees itself as responsible for creating our life, without realizing that there's so much more going on here than the ego's will.

What if you saw every experience you had as just what you needed? That would be a remarkable turnaround from how the ego sees things! But this is the truth: Every experience is the right experience. We may not understand what's right about an experience, but trusting that an experience is the right experience and seeing life as good and trustworthy transforms our experience of life.

So much of what we want, we don't really need, at least not to be happy. But we do need meaning, fulfillment, love, and a sense of belonging to something greater than ourselves to be happy. The poverty of spirit in this country, the United States, parallels the overconsumption of our lifestyle. The sense of separation from ourselves, from life, and from others instilled by the ego is painful. We try to assuage that pain with comforts and things, but these only ease the pain temporarily. Ultimately, only one thing will ease that pain, and that is seeing the truth.

The truth is really good news. The truth is we have designed our experiences to grow and to develop our talents and resources, and our experiences are very effective at accomplishing that. We do get what we need, and what we need feels very good. It feels very good to grow, to learn, to develop, and to become more kind, loving, compassionate, and wise, for these things are the result of our evolution, of living life.

The trick is we have to come to see our experiences as just what we need in order to benefit fully from them. As long as we don't see our experiences as a gift, they won't be a gift. We will stay stuck in self-pity, bitterness, resentment, and longing for something different. This is the miserable state of the ego, which doesn't appreciate life or see the wisdom and beauty in life's plan. We have to drop into the Heart to get this about life. When we've suffered enough from taking the ego's point of view, we do that. Then life can begin to change for the better.

Sometimes we do get what we want in life, and then that is

an opportunity to discover that having that isn't what we thought it would be. Our dream of getting what we want usually leaves out the negatives: We dream of success, but we don't include how demanding success is. We dream of finding our true love, but we don't include how difficult living with someone else can be. The reality is different from the dream. Getting what we want is idealized, glamorized, and never what we imagined it to be.

The greatest joy in life comes from fulfilling what you came into life to do. If that fulfillment is what you really want, you will have that. It may take a lifetime to accomplish what you came here to do, but deep happiness will be there every step of the way, and the waiting will have made the arrival all the sweeter.

On the Subject of Manifesting

Negativity is inherently a repelling state, while positivity is inherently attractive. Negativity (negative thoughts and emotions) comes from the ego and its sense of lack. When we are identified with the ego, we feel lacking, life feels lacking, and others feel lacking. The state of ego identification is a state of never having enough, of discontentment, judgment, doubt, fear, and other negative emotions. When we are identified with the ego, the world revolves around "me," "my problems," and "my life." This state is one of contraction and suffering. It is not only an uncomfortable state, but also an unattractive one.

When people are deeply identified with the ego, you can see the tension in their faces and bodies. You can hear the suffering in their voice and in what they talk about. Energetically, you can feel the negativity that accompanies this state. When we are around someone who is expressing and living out the ego's negativity, we feel drained, bored, repulsed, or bad, since their energy is often contagious. Their negative inner state gets reflected outwardly and is felt energetically, and it doesn't attract support or opportunities from others. Naturally, those in such a state want to manifest or attract love, support, opportunities, and other things, but the inner state of lack and negativity that such people are experiencing actually repels these things. Neediness is not attractive.

From this inner state of lack, many desires are born. The ego creates both the sense of lack and also the desire to manifest something to fill that lack. The solution is not to get the things, experiences, or circumstance that the ego wants to manifest, which it believes will end the lack and discontentment (but which are never enough), but rather to see that the sense of lack is a lie. That anything is lacking or necessary to be happy is the core lie that keeps the ego intact and going after one desire after another.

The antidote is to see that nothing in this moment is lacking, which is the truth. Lack is a story told by the ego, and it tells this story no matter what is happening or how much we have. When we begin to tell another story—the truth, instead of the ego's lies—our internal state changes, and we feel happy, content, loving, grateful, and generous. These feeling states not only feel good, but are also very attractive and attract to us support, love, and opportunities. Focusing on what *is* here—what you love about life, yourself, and others—rather than on what seems to be lacking is the antidote to the sense of lack and the driving neediness of the ego. It is also the key to being happy.

This positive internal state is the state of alignment with Essence, our true nature. And it brings us the true happiness, peace, and love that we all long for. The experience of our true nature is so full and complete that you won't feel the need to manifest something or make your life turn out a particular way, and yet, life will naturally bring you all the good that it intends for you. What it brings you will be aligned with the Whole, and that is a much more satisfying and fulfilling experience than getting what the *me* wants.

Find the place within you that is already full, complete, happy, and at peace with life. That fullness will draw to you and allow you to receive exactly what you need, and you will no longer feel that you have to manifest something to be happy. That's freedom, and that's what you really want. To be free of the need to manifest something in order to be happy is true happiness.

In addition to negativity repelling others and opportunities, it also creates a climate that allows, if not invites, those who are negative to be part of your life and environment. "Like attracts like" is the phrase that is often used to describe the tendency for those of a similar energy, vibration, or consciousness to be close or hang out together. The reason for this is that we as human beings like to have our self-images, beliefs, perceptions, and attitudes—our conditioning—reinforced by others. We like to be around others who are like us, even if they are negative, because they support and sustain our self-images and worldview.

Those who are very different from us in vibration or consciousness tend to cause us to question ourselves or bring out our judgments, both of which are uncomfortable. Someone who is more negative unconsciously tries to bring down someone who is more positive, and someone who is more positive unconsciously tries to bring up the other person. Fortunately, we can override any tendency to hang out with negative people once we realize what is going on by choosing otherwise, and that will help shift our consciousness. Then being more positive and being with more positive people will become more comfortable and natural. This is how evolution happens.

Those with a more positive outlook on life naturally gravitate toward those with a similar outlook and move away from those who are negative because it doesn't feel good to be around negative thinking and emotions, although more positive individuals might feel called to help uplift those who are suffering emotionally and spiritually.

Do you feel like those around you keep you down or hold you back? If so, you may be unconsciously colluding with them to keep yourself down because they reinforce your negative conditioning, self-images, and perspectives. Change these, and you will no longer find their negative presence acceptable to you. Change your inner world, and your outer world changes. When we heal our negative self-images, they stop shaping our life and our experience of life. When we stop co-creating with the ego, the false self, we are freed to co-create more with Essence. Then Essence can bring into our life what it intends for our support, happiness, and fulfillment.

If you are experiencing "attracting" negative people, you may be triggering other people's egos and negativity by something in your own attitude, demeanor, or behavior. People are our mirrors, and even people who are generally very loving and positive may mirror back the ego and its negativity to us when we are in ego. So we experience our own negativity coming back to us. When we experience those around us as being negative, we may be drawing out that negativity, just as we, when we are in a positive state, often evoke love and compliance from those around us. Our own negativity triggers negativity in others.

A simple example of this is when you complain about something, that often evokes complaints from others, possibly even aimed at you. Or if you are unfriendly, others are likely to be unfriendly too. You may think *they* are unfriendly or unpleasant without realizing that you are projecting unfriendliness yourself. Another common example is when you are angry, even generally sweet and nice people will often respond to you in anger. In this way, angry people tend to experience a world full of angry people. They create anger wherever they go.

Having said this, it is important to realize that not all difficulties are created by our negative thoughts and feelings, although many certainly are. Some difficulties are designed by our souls as catalysts for our growth or to steer us in a new direction. Difficulties are part of life. They are built into life, and no one escapes them, no matter how positive our thoughts are or how aligned with Essence we are. Essence, in fact, builds challenges into every life, but also brings us resources for overcoming them and growing from them.

When we are aligned with Essence rather than the ego, we are much better able to be happy in the midst of challenges, move through them more gracefully and wisely, and learn from them. We can come out stronger and more certain that life is meaningful and good. People who are able to do this are models for those who are caught in negativity and fear.

When we are identified with the ego, we experience both the problems caused by our negativity and the normal challenges of life, which aren't accepted by the ego and therefore aren't learned from or moved through as easily. When we are identified with the ego and its negativity, life's challenges feel overwhelming, we feel victimized, and we can't see what to do or how to respond positively, creatively, and effectively to them. Rather than strengthening and empowering us, these challenges often end up increasing our negative feelings and reinforcing any negative self-images. This is the trap that many identified with the ego experience: Their negativity keeps them from their innate wisdom and the joy of overcoming and growing from their challenges. They remain stuck in a place of discontentment, unhappiness, despair, and distrust of life.

CHAPTER 5

Your Heart's Desire

The Heart

We have the saying "your heart's desire," which is a desire that comes from deep within, not from the mind, and is felt strongly and brings great joy when that desire is attained. The ego's desires, on the other hand, are not *felt* initially. The ego's desires start out as thoughts and then become clothed in emotions, as assumptions are made and stories are told about them. This is an important distinction, which points to the main difference between the ego's desires and Essence's intentions: The ego's desires are ideas, while Essence's intentions come across as drives, impulses, intuitions, inspiration, a sense of knowing, and a feeling sense.

The Heart is another word for Essence, particularly as Essence manifests in the body. The middle of the chest, near the physical heart, is the focal point of Essence in the body. Essence can be felt there energetically, which is why Essence is sometimes referred to as the Heart. When we are aligned with Essence, we feel an expansion energetically in the area of our heart, which may also be experienced as relaxation and a release of tension that sometimes makes us sigh or say, "Ahhh." The opposite happens when we are identified with the ego: We feel a contraction or constriction of energy in the area of our heart, which may manifest as muscle tension, shallow breathing, or holding our breath. When we are identified with the ego, we feel small instead of expansive, negative instead of positive, judgmental instead of accepting, discontent instead of happy, and restless instead of peaceful.

No one wants to feel the sensations and feelings that accompany ego identification, but once we know that these uncomfortable sensations are signs of ego identification, we can make choices that will shift us into Essence. Awareness of our contracted state is the first step in moving out of ego identification and into Essence, but much more than awareness of that state is needed, or fewer people would be suffering.

Once we are aware of a state of tension and contraction, the next step is moving our attention away from our thoughts to the sensations of tension and contraction. This is counter-intuitive because we generally don't want to experience sensations such as these. However, avoidance of these sensations keeps us in ego identification. By avoiding the experience the body is having, we avoid what is real and true in the moment. Because we don't want to feel the tension and contraction in the body, we remain in our mind, which lists reasons for why we feel this way (e.g., "You're not good enough. You're not attractive enough. You're not smart enough") and offers solutions (e.g., "If you drove a nicer car, you'd look more successful, and then they'd like you"). This mental activity reinforces and perpetuates the contracted state.

Exercise: Being with the Sensations of Contraction

When you are willing to shift your attention to the contraction of energy that results from identifying with a particular thought, something very interesting happens: The sensation changes. Because the tension and contraction are caused by what your mind is telling you, shifting your attention away from your thoughts eliminates the cause of the contraction. Furthermore, focusing on the sensations of contraction brings you into your body (and out of your head) and into the moment, where you are in touch with Essence. So your energy expands, and you relax and feel happy.

Giving our attention to whatever is arising in the moment other than thoughts or feelings aligns us with Essence. When we like what's happening, giving our attention to whatever is going on is easy to do. But as soon as we don't like what's happening, we tend to get involved in our thoughts. The egoic mind is in the business of coming up with reasons to not be present to what is going on, and it often succeeds in shifting our attention away from what's actually happening to thoughts *about* what's happening or to thoughts that are entirely unrelated to what's happening. For example, when you're watching a sunset, the mind might interrupt with warnings about it getting colder soon, followed by memories when you were cold, and then memories of another time that had nothing to do with sunsets or cool evenings.

The egoic mind often offers seemingly helpful advice about something that's happening, but before we know it, the mind is running on about the past, the future, and anything else it can get us to listen to. The egoic mind's purpose is to get us to listen to it, and for that, what it says doesn't have to be relevant or even make sense. In fact, irrelevant or nonsensical information often grabs our attention more than relevant and sensible information. The mind tries to entertain us with nonsense, gossip, memories, fantasies, and interesting factoids.

We are entertained to some extent by the fabrications of the egoic mind, but that entertainment costs us dearly. When we allow ourselves to be entertained by this aspect of the mind, we get sucked into the ego's world, which is a world of negativity, jealousy, gossip, judgments, one-upmanship, pettiness, and meanness. Before you know it, you've identified with that negativity, pettiness, and meanness, and that negativity causes you to contract and feel bad about yourself.

How can you love yourself when you feel negative, petty, and mean-spirited? Loving ourselves isn't easy when we are caught up in the egoic mind. We assume that loving ourselves means loving the ego. However, the ego isn't particularly lovable. Loving ourselves isn't about loving the part of us that is mean and petty, but about realizing our true nature, which is not mean and petty. It's easy to love ourselves when we are aligned with Essence, and it's not easy to love ourselves when we aren't. The good news is that the real you is completely lovable, and the *you* that isn't so lovable is the false you. The false self just needs to be recognized and accepted for what it is — false. The way we love the false self is by accepting it as part of the human condition and having compassion for this very human aspect of ourselves, but not acting it out or giving voice to it.

The ego is the perpetuator of human suffering. It has a role and purpose in creating the drama that drives life. However, once we become aware of the falseness of the egoic mind, we can opt out of the drama it creates. The game can be over once we see what's going on and choose to stop playing. Seeing the truth about the egoic mind is important, but choosing to stop playing, stop identifying with that aspect of the mind, is more important. Seeing the truth only gets us so far. At some point, we have to choose to give our allegiance (our attention) to Essence and its intuitions, drives, and inspiration instead of to the egoic mind.

Listening to the Heart

The Heart is not difficult to hear. We listen to it all the time. It just doesn't speak to us in words, like the mind, so we have to listen with something other than our mind. When the mind is quiet, we are able to hear the Heart, which is often drowned out by the mind. Meditation is valuable because it helps quiet the mind, and it teaches us to detach from the mind so that Essence can be heard in the way that it speaks, which is primarily through the intuition, but also through urges to act and feelings of elation, excitement, and joy.

Intuition is something that develops over our many lifetimes. Our default position, you could say, is listening to the chatter of the egoic mind. That's what we naturally do, but evolution teaches us that there's something wiser to listen to. Through trial and error, we learn to interpret our intuition and use it correctly. Eventually, our intuition becomes so strong and clear that it overpowers the egoic mind. Then Essence has a real chance of being embodied and expressed through us. Before then, embodying Essence more fully is difficult to do because the ego has a stronger voice.

Fortunately, there are things we can do to develop our intuition. One of the biggest hurdles is not admitting that intuition exists. Because many don't consider the possibility of listening to something other than the mind, they don't notice intuitions when they do arise. Or if they do, they discount or disbelieve them. So the first step in developing our intuition is to want to develop it, which requires recognizing its existence and valuing it. To realize the value of intuition, looking into your own experience may be helpful.

Your intuition has undoubtedly served you well many times. It may have even saved your life, or at least saved you a lot of trouble. You may have had the experience of a voice popping into your head, telling you to stop or look, or giving you other sound advice. During emergencies or critical situations, our intuition often comes through the mind that way. When that happens, the message is usually no more than a few words, and the experience feels very different than our usual thoughts. Intuitive messages are brief, to the point, and feel right, while our thoughts tend to chatter on and leave us feeling confused or contracted.

You've also probably had experiences of just knowing or feeling something so strongly that you had to follow that. These knowings and feelings tend to be associated with energetic sensations in the chest or midsection, which is why they are often called gut feelings. These instances tend to get our attention because gut feelings have a numinous quality that distinguishes them from thoughts or emotions.

One of the most important things you can do to develop your intuition is to pay attention to instances like these. Giving these types of communication our attention, affirms that we value them, which increases the likelihood they will recur. The more you pay attention to your intuition, the more you will be communicated to this way. You can take this a step further and ask for more communications of this type, and you'll receive them: "Ask and you shall receive." Asking opens the door for spiritual help to flow to us.

Essence also often uses other people to deliver its messages and communicate its intentions, so be sure to pay attention to anything that other people say to you that has a similar ring or feeling as your own intuition. Pay attention to when your words or other people's words have a ring of truth to them because that's a sign that they come from Essence.

Essence has plans and intentions for every human being, and it makes these intentions known in various ways. However, if you are focused on your thoughts, desires, and fantasies, you may not pick up on Essence's intentions, and then you will miss out on the fulfillment that comes from following them. Unlike the ego's goals, Essence's goals are meaningful and intrinsically rewarding. When we are following Essence's intentions, we don't need the promise of a future reward to motivate us. We are naturally driven to fulfill Essence's intentions, when we are aware of them, and doing so brings joy.

This is one of the biggest differences between the ego and Essence: The ego does things for future rewards, while Essence does things that feel rewarding. When we are doing something that feels rewarding, we are embodying Essence. While the ego often pushes itself and motivates itself with external rewards, with Essence, the reward is in the doing. So if you want to know what your Heart's desire is, look to the things that you love to do, things that no one has to tell you to do or reward you to do. What is your Heart's desire?

Summary: How to Develop Your Intuition

1. Acknowledge the existence and value of intuition. Affirm your desire to develop it.

2. Recall times when you were aware of your intuition and

when your intuition was helpful. What did that feel like? Notice when you have that same feeling, and pay attention to that feeling. Trust it.

3. Ask (pray) for more intuitive communications.

4. Pay attention to anything that other people say to you that has a similar ring of truth as your own intuition.

5. Meditate to develop detachment from your egoic mind.

6. Notice where your joy is. Joy is a signal of a yes from Essence.

The Heart Loves Love

The Heart loves. It loves and accepts everything that happens in life because it loves life. However, although the Heart accepts everything, it moves us and life toward love. The Heart allows the ego to move away from love, but the Heart is always moving us toward love. Eventually the Heart wins out, and we all end up feeling love, gratitude, and appreciation for life and for all that life has brought us, for that is how the Heart, or Essence, feels in every moment.

The Heart desires love above all else. It isn't willing to exchange money, safety, power, prestige, success, or anything else for love. Love is the Heart's priority, and that is how we can tell Essence from the ego. The ego isn't willing to choose love over these things unless it sees love as an avenue to these things.

In any moment, the Heart is choosing love, while the ego is likely to be choosing something else. What are you choosing?

When we are unaware of the possibility of choosing love or when we are unaccustomed to choosing love, we may not see that we have a choice. And yet every moment holds the possibility of either choosing love or choosing the ego's way of being and seeing. What is the loving choice in this moment? What would Essence do? When those questions become a part of every moment, life flows and flowers.

The loving choice draws love to it, which is all we have ever wanted anyway. Love is the most powerfully attractive force in the universe, more powerful than beauty, power, wealth, success, or anything else we might want. When we choose love, we align ourselves with Essence, with the Heart. We drop instantly into Essence, where other qualities of Essence, such as gratitude, peace, contentment, and happiness, can be felt.

This sounds so simple, but if dropping into Essence were easy, there would be much more love in the world. The reason doing this isn't easy is that we are programmed to pay attention to the egoic mind, and giving attention to anything is the same as choosing it. Whatever we give our attention to, we identify with. If we give our attention to love, we identify with love, and if we give our attention to our thoughts, we identify with (i.e., believe) them.

Choosing love requires consciously choosing to put our attention on the present moment and on the qualities of Essence instead of on our thoughts, and that takes awareness and the will to go against our programming. Once we are convinced that our programming, or conditioning, isn't worth paying attention to, giving our attention to the moment isn't so difficult. The challenge is that we are programmed to believe our thoughts and follow our conditioning.

Choosing love requires seeing beyond the ego's desires, needs, and conditioning. The ego only knows what it wants, what it feels it needs, what it believes, what it was taught, and what has worked in the past. When we are identified with the egoic mind, we make choices and act on the basis of the ego's needs, its knowledge, and its perceptions, which often doesn't result in the best response. Only Essence has the wisdom to know what is best for each situation, not the ego.

Even trying to answer the question, "What does Essence want?" might not give us the answer. We might only get the ego's answer to that question. Still, this question is worth asking because doing so interrupts the automatic identification with the egoic mind that is our default position long enough to allow the possibility of Essence to inform us of the truth in Essence's own way.

Asking that question stops us momentarily and invites us to listen, and listening is key to aligning with Essence and with love. Because we are usually busy listening to the egoic mind, we don't hear Essence, but if our involvement with the mind is interrupted with that question, the answer may come forth from Essence. The answer isn't likely to show up as words, but as spontaneous action in accordance with love or as a sense of knowing what action would promote love.

The Heart Loves to Create

The Heart loves love, and it also loves to create. In addition to learning to love, one of the purposes of our existence is to create. We are here to be creators, so our Heart's desire is also to create. How and what we create is different for everyone, but we all create and enjoy creating in many ways: Some of the many things people create are: children, houses, homes, companies, buildings, machines, financial plans, websites, meals, art, music, poetry, dance, books, games, fashion, hair designs, athletic bodies, governments, policies, laws, lectures, workshops, schools, love, peace, and philosophies. The list is endless.

In truth, everything we do is a form of creation: how we comb our hair, how we speak, how we butter our bread, how we play with a child, how we walk, how we pet a dog, how we dance, how we make love, and how we dress. Even these simple, basic things are done in a way that is unique to each of us and therefore creative. Our uniqueness is an expression of the creativity of the Divine.

In every moment, Essence is creating through us, usually in conjunction with the ego. Sometimes the ego blocks creativity or takes it in a very different direction from Essence, but even then, creativity is being expressed. Essence uses our body, mind, and talents to create in its own unique way through us. Essence doesn't know exactly what we will create, but it inspires us to try new things, explore new possibilities, and expand our understanding and talents. It takes great pleasure in evolving us in these ways, for every new thing we try is a learning experience for us and for Essence.

We make it possible for the Divine to create and explore in this reality, and the Divine takes great joy in doing so. This joy can be felt in every moment. It's the joy that the Divine feels in experiencing and exploring life through us. Even in the simplest creative act, there is great joy. Essence enjoys doing even simple things because even they are intrinsically rewarding.

Doing simple things isn't interesting to the ego, however. The ego overlooks the value and enjoyment of doing simple things, and it takes us out of the moment with thoughts about what we're doing or thoughts about something else. These thoughts take us away from the experience of joy in the moment and land us in the unreal world of the egoic mind, where worry, negativity, judgment, and discontent prevail. The world of Essence and the world of the egoic mind coexist, and we can choose which world we will live in, but first, we have to be aware that there is a choice.

Because the joy of the moment is subtle and discounted by the egoic mind, it is easy to overlook. To experience it, we have to purposely pay attention to it instead of the mind. The more we pay attention to that subtle joy, the more easily it is felt. The ego doesn't give this joy a chance to be felt because as soon as we touch into it, the ego pulls us away with a thought. The ego doesn't want us to land in Essence because then it loses us, and it has to work hard to get us back. The egoic mind can become very insistent when it's threatened with being ignored. Notice how desperately it tries to get your attention whenever you stop giving it your attention.

When we give our attention to the moment, Essence uses us to express itself in the world. Essence is friendly to others, makes us smile, offers helpful advice, cheers someone up, makes someone laugh, or it may create a bouquet or something else of beauty. Essence responds appropriately and lovingly in every situation, and it urges us to do whatever we need to do to take care of ourselves and keep ourselves safe. Essence naturally stretches the body when it needs stretching, and it inspires us to buy and eat healthy foods. It encourages us to rest when we are tired and to exercise when we need that.

All of these acts are creative because they are expressions of Essence in the moment to suit the moment. These acts aren't planned or thought about, but come spontaneously out of the moment. Essence responds with what the moment calls for, and that spontaneous response is a creative act. Essence creates responses and actions, which in turn, create friends, connections, a healthy body, and in many other ways, a good, fulfilling life because living life that way is fulfilling.

In addition to the creativity of everyday acts, Essence also often likes to try its hand at creating in the usual ways. It will use whatever talents we have in a creative way: If you love cooking, Essence will try new recipes, and it may invent some too. If you love to sing, it will experiment with your voice, and it may even write some songs. If you are interested in commerce, it may give you new ideas for businesses or new ways to run an old business.

Everything we love to do and are good at is a potential avenue for Essence's creative expression. Whatever you love doing is where you can be the most creative and where being creative can be the most fulfilling for you because that is the area you were meant to be creative in. Some people don't consider themselves creative because they aren't creative in the ways that other people are, but everyone has areas where their creativity is naturally expressed.

The more you notice how Essence is already creating through you, the more that kind of creativity will happen. Sometimes we miss a creative opportunity by blocking our creativity with negative thoughts and judgments. Because the ego values outcomes and rewards above processes, it often discounts creative acts unless they result in recognition, money, and other things the ego wants. With Essence, however, life is all about the journey. The act of creating is its own reward, and no other reward is necessary.

The beauty is that every moment is creative in some way. As a result, every moment has the potential to be fulfilling if we are willing to stay in the moment and experience Essence's joy in expressing itself. Watch and see what Essence will do next. It will be a surprise to you and to Essence, but that's what is fun about creativity. The fun is in the surprise of the creative process. Creating is much more fun than thinking, planning, and evaluating, which is the ego's alternative to Essence's spontaneous expression.

Exercise: Exploring Your Creativity

How do you create? Take a moment and contemplate the many ways that you are creative. How does Essence create through you? How does it create through you most often? What are your creative gifts? What do you enjoy doing most? Doing that is important for your fulfillment. If you feel joy in doing something, then you were meant to do that. That activity is how Essence is experiencing joy through your unique body-mind. The more you do the things you enjoy, the more you will uncover the possibilities in that activity. You are meant to unfold yourself in some way through those activities that are most joyful.

The Heart Loves Experience

Essence loves experiencing as much as it loves loving and creating. When love and creativity aren't happening, experience is still happening, and Essence loves that. When we are lost in the egoic mind and having that experience, Essence even loves that. When we are experiencing the results of the ego's choices, Essence loves that too. There isn't an experience you can have that Essence doesn't love. Essence loves being alive through us, no matter what is happening.

Essence's love for experience is available in every moment just by noticing this love, this subtle joy. But when the ego doesn't like what's happening, noticing Essence's love for life isn't so easy. When the ego is unhappy with an experience, which happens a lot, it lists everything it doesn't like about the experience and nothing it might like. The ego leaves out the positives, even the positives it recognizes. This is how the ego builds a case to support being unhappy.

The ego loves to spin a negative story of woe, "poor me," and "ain't it awful." This gives the ego the sense of being somebody, even if it's somebody who is struggling, victimized, or unhappy. The ego would rather be an unhappy somebody than nobody. The ego's list of problems gives it a sense of being special and a story to tell others. Negative stories are not only a way of getting attention and help from others, but also of engaging others. Sharing negative stories is the ego's way of connecting with others.

Many people form an identity around their problems and difficulties. They see themselves as someone who has a problem. It may be a longstanding problem or whatever problem is most current. Many people turn even the normal kinds of problems into a reason to feel sorry for themselves. In dwelling on the negatives, they make themselves and everyone around them miserable. We call people like these drama queens, but we all have that same potential for drama because we all have an ego.

Any experience we are having also has many positives, which the ego may not know of or doesn't acknowledge. The ego doesn't know the value that an unpleasant experience may have for us spiritually. The ego doesn't take into account the value of difficulties, only their unpleasantness. It overlooks the psychological and spiritual benefits that come from challenging circumstances. Essence, on the other hand, relishes challenges for the growth they provide. If Essence didn't want growth, then growth and the difficulties that catalyze growth wouldn't be part of life.

It's no mistake that challenges and difficulties happen.

Some difficulties are the result of bad choices, but many are just part of life, part of having a human body. No one escapes certain challenges, such as illness, pain, aging, and death. The ego pretends it's more special than others and that it shouldn't have those same difficulties. The ego is in denial over its humanity because it doesn't want to admit its vulnerability. It knows the body will die someday, but it doesn't want to believe that, so it pretends that death won't happen. The ego feels that death shouldn't happen, and it fears it.

The ego is opposed to death, as it is to most of what happens in life. It opposes even the inevitable because that is the ego's basic stance toward life. That opposition only makes death and other challenges more difficult. That opposition to life, that resistance to the way things are, is the ego's main defense against life. The ego defends against life by resisting life, but doing that doesn't make the ego safer or less vulnerable. All the complaints in the world don't add up to anything. They don't change a thing. They are impotent in the face of life, which ultimately has its way with us.

As obvious as this truth is when it is pointed out, it is not obvious to the ego, which continues to complain about and resist so much of what is happening. The ego is just unhappy, and nothing will change that. Fortunately, we don't have to get rid of the ego or our thoughts to be happy. We can be happy in spite of the ego's unhappy state if we learn to ignore the egoic mind. Just as you might avoid people who complain too much, you can learn to ignore the negative mind. It has nothing to offer.

It's too easy to complain, to find the negative in a situation. Finding negatives is easy because this is a world of duality, of pleasant and unpleasant, hot and cold, clean and dirty, pretty and ugly. Complaints assume that one half of the coin—the negative—shouldn't be there, which is like saying the sky shouldn't be there. Life is the way it is. There's no use arguing with the way life is. But arguing with life is what the egoic mind does, and it convinces us that it is serving us by doing that.

When we are identified with the ego, we believe the mind's assertions that things should be different, and believing that lie makes us angry. We feel victimized by life because we believe the mind when it tells us that life shouldn't be the way it is, people shouldn't be the way they are, and nature shouldn't be the way it is. Life is the way it is, and who are we to argue with it? The ego's position is an arrogant one. The ego claims to know better than life itself what is right and good.

Essence loves the messiness, unpredictability, and challenge of life. The Divine made life just the way it is, including the ego. The Divine allows the egoic mind to do what it does and even to create the suffering it creates with its wrong beliefs and attitudes. The Divine loves the growth that comes with this world of duality. No other situation could provide such growth.

The Heart Loves Growth

One of the reasons the Heart loves every experience is that it loves the growth that comes from each experience. Essence loves growth because it loves to learn, and we feel that love for learning whenever we learn something. Learning is inherently fulfilling. It's entertaining, it's fun, it makes us happy, it develops us, it improves our life, and it can even save our life. We love to learn because it is essential to growth and to life.

Growth comes out of experience, no matter what the experience is. Every experience is somewhat challenging because it requires an immediate response, and the result of that response is unknown. So every moment is an experiment with an uncertain outcome. Essence loves the unpredictability of life, but the ego doesn't. That unpredictability is a big reason why the ego wants to leave the moment. Thinking about what's happening, instead of experiencing it, is the ego's way of trying to gain some control over life. The ego's conclusions about an experience are an attempt to define the experience and predict the outcome. The ego puts every experience into a conceptual box by telling a story about it. But that story is never complete enough and leaves out so much, particularly what growth, insight, wisdom, compassion, and love might come from that experience.

The ego spins stories about an experience according to its values, which are primarily success, security, safety, money, prestige, power, fun, pleasure, ease, and comfort. If the experience doesn't measure up in one or more of these ways, the experience is deemed bad; if it does, it is deemed good. These values aren't sufficient to measure the value of an experience or to define it, but the ego ignores the complexities and subtleties of life. The ego paints experiences as either good or bad, meaning good or bad for *it*.

When the moment is just experienced, stripped of all labels, evaluations, stories, and opinions, the moment is juicy and real, no matter what is happening. The aliveness of every moment can be felt if it isn't drowned out by the evaluations and stories that inevitably accompany each moment. By giving our attention to the aliveness instead of to the ego's stories, judgments, and evaluations about whatever is happening, the feeling of aliveness increases and the egoic mind's voice decreases. The volume of the mind is only loud because we give the egoic mind power by listening to it. Whatever we give our attention to stands out in our awareness, so if we give our attention to the aliveness, that aliveness will stand out instead of our thoughts.

The mind discounts the aliveness, which is the energetic sensation that accompanies Essence. When we are aligned with Essence, we feel this aliveness. It is how we experience our true nature. When we feel more deeply into this aliveness instead of discount it, we discover that it contains everything we have always wanted: peace, joy, happiness, contentment.

You are not a body-mind or even a personality. You are what is aware of and alive as the body-mind and personality. Awareness, or Consciousness, is attached to that body-mind and personality, and it animates the body-mind and personality, but it isn't limited to the body-mind and personality. We discover this at death, when Awareness remains, while its attachment to the body-mind is severed.

To a large extent, growth involves discovering a truer voice than the egoic mind's voice. This growth is inevitable because to remain identified with the egoic mind would mean never escaping suffering. If it weren't for learning, endless suffering would be our fate. But we learn as a result of our suffering, and that learning takes us away from the ego and into our true nature. This evolution is unstoppable. Even those entrenched in the ego do grow and open up to Essence—to love—to some extent even in just one lifetime.

Not a lifetime goes by in which growth doesn't occur. This may be hard to believe in considering the most vicious killers. However, learning continues even after death. Much of our most important learning takes place after every lifetime, when we are guided by spiritual beings to review our previous lifetime from the perspective of those whom we affected. Dramatic conversions often happen as a result of this life review because we have more access to objectivity, understanding, and compassion after death than when we did when we were alive.

The life review can have a powerful and lasting effect, one that changes our behavior for the next incarnation and beyond. No one wants to stay separate from love, and the life review makes it apparent that life is all about love. How we keep ourselves separate from love with our ideas about ourselves and about others becomes clear, and this realization can bring about a permanent transformation.

The Heart Loves Discovery

If life were not so mysterious, there would be nothing to discover. The joy in discovery is proof that life is intended to be a mystery. The Divine created this mystery for us to solve. The egoic mind tries to solve the mystery of life, but it can only be solved by the Heart because it can only be understood by the Heart.

Part of what makes life mysterious is the immensity of what is unknown. There's so little in the present moment that we know to be true. What is real is only what we know to be true right here, right now. With everything else, we are pretending to know, mostly without realizing we are doing that. We pretend to know the sun will rise tomorrow, but we don't really know that. We make assumptions about what will happen based on what is happening or on what has happened — but we don't really know what will happen. In fact, life often surprises us. Everything that happens, happens all of sudden, without warning: All of a sudden you sneeze, all of a sudden the doorbell rings, all of a sudden someone dies, all of a sudden you trip, all of a sudden someone says something, all of a sudden you decide to do something.

Although the future rarely complies with the ego's plans and ideas, the ego continues to plan and think about the future.

The ego is convinced that all this thinking and planning is necessary and important. The ego doesn't see the lack of connection between what it thinks and what actually happens. This may be because what the ego thinks does occasionally coincide with what happens, and that's powerfully reinforcing to the ego's belief that thinking matters.

The reason the ego thinks about the future as much as it does is because it doesn't like the uncertainty of not knowing what will happen. Thinking is the ego's way of trying to gain some control over this mystery. The ego's refusal to see the truth—that its planning and thinking about the future don't matter—is the ego's defense against its own impotence. It pretends to be able to affect the future, even in the face of evidence to the contrary, because that's how the ego copes with not knowing.

The ego is uncomfortable with not knowing because not knowing makes it feel unsafe, and safety is one of its biggest concerns. Pretending to know, even when it doesn't, is how the ego attempts to keep us safe, and we tend to believe the ego. We don't really question the ego's plans and daydreams of the future. We tend to accept them as valid and useful because we are programmed to view our thoughts that way. We believe our thoughts, we live by them, and we trust them, even though they have let us down more than they've been true. Our thoughts still seem better than nothing. After all, what are we left with if thoughts can't be believed?

The answer to that question is that we are left with a big, gaping void, a mystery. We are left with not knowing very much. Of course, we have never been able to know very much, even when the mind pretended otherwise, so we haven't really lost anything if we stop listening to the egoic mind. We've never really known what was going to happen next, much less days or weeks or years from now. We just don't know. That's the truth and the reality. We don't like this, but it's true. To break through our programming, we need to remind ourselves of this again and again because pretending to know keeps us from being in contact with what we do know, which is what is real right here, right now.

If listening to the mind's ideas about life were harmless, there would be no need to stop doing it. Our thoughts are entertaining, but that entertainment comes at a high price. The price we pay for listening to our thoughts is a lack of contact with Essence, and Essence is the source of happiness, love, peace, and contentment. What we exchange happiness, love, peace, and contentment for are thoughts *about* life. Essence allows us to live in the ego's unreal mental world for as long as we choose, but eventually we become disillusioned with the mind because we catch on that it can't deliver what it promises.

Fortunately, something does love the mysteriousness of life. It finds it exciting, delicious, adventuresome, delightful, interesting, fun, and beautiful. Essence loves the mystery because it's a way for it to have the experience of discovery, which is very joyful. What fun we have watching a movie and not knowing how it will end! Those are the movies we really love, not the predictable ones. We love the mystery then. This is exactly how Essence feels about life, and we feel this way too when we are in touch with Essence.

Being in touch with Essence gives us the same distance and objectivity toward life that watching a movie does. We love the mystery when it's not affecting our sense of safety, when the mystery is affecting the characters on the screen instead of us. When we are in contact with Essence, life isn't taken so personally because we know we aren't the character we are playing, so enjoying the mystery is much easier. Not knowing is exciting and interesting instead of scary. The unknown is scary to the ego because not knowing makes the ego feel unsafe, and feeling unsafe isn't fun and exciting to the ego. But to Essence, which knows nothing but safety, the unknown is fun.

While the ego wants safety and knowing, the Heart loves the mystery just the way it is, with all of its surprises and the opportunities for creativity, experience, growth, and discovery that those surprises provide. The mysteriousness of life makes creativity, growth, and love possible, since creativity, growth, and love are all necessary to successfully negotiate life's surprises. All the things the Heart desires, it desires for a reason. It desires love, creativity, experience, growth, and not knowing because these are the ingredients that make life what it is and what it is intended to be.

CHAPTER 6

Finding Happiness in Whatever Is Happening

Being happy no matter what is happening only requires that we want what Essence wants—love, peace, unity, experience, growth, challenge, not knowing, discovery, and creativity—more than we want what the ego wants. Essence loves reality because reality provides all of these things. Essence accepts reality the way it is because Essence intended reality to be that way. Finding happiness isn't a matter of giving up desires, but of giving our attention to the desires that will bring true happiness.

We choose what we desire by giving our attention to it. Whatever you are giving your attention to is what you desire. Are you sure that's what you really want? Usually we give our attention to a thought about something we want, even though thinking about what we want doesn't manifest it (which is our hope). Thinking about what we want takes us out of the moment, where contentment, peace, and true happiness are available and where it is possible to discover Essence's intentions for our life by paying attention to how Essence is moving us *now*.

If you focus on wanting something long enough, you may find yourself taking action to try to bring that into your life. But is that desire worth your energy and time? If that desire comes from the ego, it may not be worth your time and energy. Going after what you *think* you want may result in getting what you want, but is that what you really want? Instead, if you give your attention to what is arising in the moment, you will discover what Essence wants, and Essence will move you to create the life you were meant to live.

Wanting to Be Happy More Than to Be Somebody

This may sound obvious, but you have to want happiness to have it. You have to want to be happy more than you want to be *you* (the egoic self), with all your stories, beliefs, opinions, judgments, dreams, and memories. Happiness will never be found in being *you*, not even in being a better, improved version of *you*. It can only be found in losing your self—losing all thoughts that relate to the *me*, the false self—and finding your true self.

This is the price to be paid for happiness. Happiness isn't attained by improving ourselves or by working harder or by having more money, more beauty, more success, or more friends because we won't ever have enough of these things to make the ego happy. As long as we are focused on the *me*, we won't find happiness because the ego doesn't know how to be happy. Only in realizing we are not the ego—we are not who we *think* we are—will we find true happiness. When we discover who we really are, we don't need anything to make us happy because we already are happy.

Who we really are (Essence) has always been happy, and it has always been possible for us to feel that happiness.

Whenever we stop thinking or stop paying attention to our thoughts, we experience peace, contentment, happiness, and joy. Thoughts about ourselves are the only thing in the way of happiness. Involvement with the *me* (the false, or egoic, self) is the cause of suffering. The *me* and suffering go hand in hand: We can't have one without the other. So the choice is clear: We can be involved with all our thoughts about *me* and suffer, or we can be in the moment and ignore our thoughts and be happy.

Although this choice is clear, making this choice isn't easy because we love our stories, beliefs, opinions, judgments, memories, fantasies, desires, and other ideas. When we are identified with them, we are loving them more than we love to love—more than we love Essence. When it comes to choosing between our ideas and love, we often choose our ideas. We want to be who we *think* we are more than we want to stop suffering. But there's no blame in that. We are programmed to love our thoughts. Nevertheless, the time eventually comes to wake up out of our programming and make another choice. When that time comes, Essence's pull becomes stronger.

This is the point that most of you who are reading this are at, or it's likely that you wouldn't be reading this. It's time to see that you don't have to suffer. There's another way to live. But you have to choose this new way of living—you have to choose to be in the moment and not in your thoughts—and doing so isn't so easy because of our programming. The hardest thing about making that choice is that it has to be made again and again in every new moment.

We are never done making this choice because the ego continues to play its role even long after we have realized who we really are. Although the egoic mind weakens the less we pay attention to it, it continues to tantalize us with stories, judgments, opinions, fantasies, memories, and desires. Even when we recognize these thoughts for what they are, they may still draw us in for some time. How long this continues is different for everyone, but many who have seen the truth never leave the ego entirely behind.

It doesn't matter how strong the egoic mind's voice is as long as we ignore it. We can't change the programming, but we can change our relationship to the programming: We notice the programming instead of respond automatically to it. When we do that, the programming weakens. This is the way out of the suffering the ego causes, and no one but you can do this choosing for you. Waking up isn't easy, but neither is suffering. However, suffering is our default position, and there's some comfort in that position because it's so familiar. So we are pulled in one direction or the other until eventually Essence wins out.

Moving back and forth between the ego and Essence can go on for a very long time, even an entire lifetime. Without the spiritual understanding needed to get beyond the ego, it's a formidable opponent. Once we understand how the ego operates and maintains suffering, however, choosing Essence over the ego becomes easier. Furthermore, the more you do this, the stronger Essence's voice becomes. The desire to awaken and to be done with the ego and its suffering becomes stronger than the desire to indulge your thoughts, and then you are on your way to freedom and happiness.

Seeking Happiness Through Awakening

When it's time to awaken, the desire to awaken becomes very strong. This desire comes from Essence and manifests as a deep longing to return Home. Sometimes the ego turns this longing into a story about how badly we want to awaken but can't or about some spiritual experience that seemed like an awakening or about how we will never awaken. These stories about awakening are just that—stories the ego tells—and they only result in suffering. Essence spurs awakening on through the Heart: through longing, burning love, and devotion. Sometimes spiritual experiences happen during this phase, which strengthen the commitment to awakening.

Essence doesn't tell stories about awakening, but the ego does. The mind is full of ideas about awakening. The mind thinks awakening should happen a certain way, look a certain way, and feel a certain way. The mind has gathered these ideas from books, teachers, and others on the spiritual path, many of which are incorrect. These misconceptions cause a lot of confusion: Sometimes spiritual experiences are mistaken for awakening, and when awakening does occur, that isn't always recognized.

The ego is tricky, and it's no less involved in spiritual matters than anything else. The ego may pretend to be awake or enlightened by taking on a spiritual tone of voice and appearance and mimicking spiritual teachers. Essence isn't fooled by this, so when we are aligned with Essence, we can tell if someone is speaking from the Heart. However, if we are identified with the ego, like most people, telling if someone is awakened or not may not be so easy.

Usually the desire to awaken comes from Essence, but that desire is often co-opted by the ego, and then it can become a source of suffering. If you are suffering over not being awake, you can be sure the ego is causing that suffering. Essence doesn't suffer over not being awake because not being awake isn't a problem for Essence. But for the ego who travels in spiritual circles, awakening is one more goal for the ego to achieve, and failure to achieve it is especially painful. Often the spiritual seeker has given up other goals for this one true goal: awakening or enlightenment. To not achieve this goal, then, is particularly painful. The ego may want to awaken more than anything else because not achieving awakening is deemed the greatest failure of all and proof of its unworthiness. Failing to awaken can be a cause for great unhappiness for the ego.

The way out of suffering over not awakening is to see that spiritual seeking can be just one more form of seeking outside ourselves for happiness and, as such, spiritual seeking is bound to cause suffering. The truth is the ego can't awaken and the ego can't do anything about this. The real you is already awake and enjoying life. All you need to see is this: Who you *think* you are doesn't exist. Stop pretending you are this idea about yourself, this false self, this nonexistent self. Stop suffering over this story of *you* that you made up. Stop telling this story. Stop listening to this story. Stop believing this story. And what you have left is just this simple, ordinary, yet stunningly beautiful moment stripped of all the glamour and drama of the ego.

Seeking happiness is different from choosing happiness. Seeking is just more of the ego doing what it does: trying to get something. Choosing happiness means choosing something other than the ego and its seeking and striving. Choosing happiness means choosing to be in the present moment just as it is and not running from it or trying to change it. Choosing happiness is a decision to love what is instead of rejecting it, thinking about it, or ignoring it. Loving what is, is just allowing whatever is to be the way it is, for now, because that will undoubtedly change.

Wanting to Love More Than to Be Right

The desire to be right is one of the ego's strongest desires because being right is felt to be closely tied to survival. Being right puts us on top, and that's where the ego wants to be because the ego thinks that being on top will keep it safe. Again and again, the ego will choose being right over love and connection with others. This tendency to make being right more important than love is what makes relationships so difficult. When people in a relationship are ego identified, both want to be right, and that's especially impossible when no one is actually right!

The reason that no one is actually right is because disagreements are based on conditioning, and conditioning is simply different beliefs. Everyone thinks their beliefs are right. However, there is no absolute truth when it comes to beliefs, only relative truth. Conditioning is conditioning, and all conditioning bears the stamp of the ego. Conditioning is made up of generalizations, beliefs that have been passed on, truisms, cultural and religious training, and other acquired ideas. When we are attached to our conditioning and to being right, we argue about things like the right way to make the bed or wash the dishes. Getting the other person to do things our way becomes more important than loving that person and accepting that we are all different.

Essence loves our differences, or we wouldn't be the way we are. Life wouldn't be what it is if we weren't different from each other. What an amazing thing it is that each of us is so unique! However, the ego feels threatened by these differences, and so it is uncomfortable with them. We are designed to both love others and disagree with them. It's part of our evolution to learn to lovingly disagree, which requires that we hold our differences more lightly than the ego is used to doing.

Wanting to be right is not a worthwhile desire, and that has to be seen. This desire is the ego doing what egos do. Choosing love over being right is the choice that brings happiness because choosing love over our conditioning shifts us out of the ego's world and into Essence's. Essence chooses love because Essence is moving all of life toward love. Whenever we choose love over being right, or any other value of the ego, we drop into Essence and immediately experience the love, peace, joy, and contentment of Essence.

By using our will to choose love instead of following our programming, we evoke love. As soon as we give our attention to love, we land in love. And what could be better than that? When you make this choice often enough, you discover that being loving and accepting feels much better than being right. The ego gets some smug pleasure from being right, but that bit of pleasure can't compare with the good feeling that comes from loving.

Noticing that you have a choice is key to making the right choice. When we are involved with others, we often go unconscious and respond automatically from the ego. Being in relationship is challenging even to those who are very conscious and aware because the ego is easily triggered in relationship. As soon as we open our mouths, we tend to give voice to the ego and its thoughts, without evaluating those thoughts first. What we often voice are our opinions and judgments, all of which are likely better left unsaid. The ego's opinions and judgments don't serve our relationships any more than they serve us. Opinions and judgments are generally a way we try to prove to others that we are right. When we pay close attention to our interactions with others, we discover that much of what we say is an attempt to know something or to be right, which is how the ego tries to be superior.

Another desire can replace the desire to be right and to be superior, and that is the desire for love and unity. You can choose to not speak the ego's divisive judgments, opinions, and beliefs. The loving choice is often to *not* speak. You choose to not give your attention to the ego's judgments, opinions, and beliefs because giving your attention to them doesn't support love. When you make the choice to ignore and not give voice to such thoughts, you are choosing Essence's desire for love over the ego's desire to be right. Here is an exercise to help you to make this positive choice:

Exercise: Wanting to Be Right

Notice how much the ego wants to be right, even about things that don't matter. Most opinions and judgments are an expression of the drive to be right. Your "superior" opinion or judgment is how you try to make yourself superior to others. It's funny how we assume that our opinions and judgments are superior because they're ours. This is true of everyone and causes a lot of conflict in relationships. Do you really know that your opinion or judgment is true? We express our opinions as if they were the last word, and so does everyone else.

Notice how much energy and conversation are taken up by everyone trying to prove that their viewpoint is the right one. Notice how contracted you feel when you are expressing an opinion or judgment, and then notice what a relief it is to let go of that position. Relaxation and expansion is your natural state, while contraction is the state of ego identification.

Wanting to Not Know More Than to Know

We torture ourselves trying to know things we can't know, and we get angry because we don't know things we want to know. Most of all, we want to know what's going to happen in the story of *me*. Will I get what I want or not? Wanting to know what's going to happen is very intimately tied with our desires: We want to know what's going to happen because we want what we want to happen. Sometimes we want what we want so much that it hurts, and sometimes we fear what we don't want so much that it hurts. We suffer immensely over our desires and over wondering if life will ever be the way we want it to be.

Underlying all this desiring and fearing is the assumption that we can get what we want or ward off what we don't want by thinking about it. It's not that our actions don't contribute to creating our future — they do — but there are so many unknowns in any situation that we really can't be sure if we will get what we want or don't want until we do or we don't.

Nothing we do can give us that surety — not thinking, planning, or dreaming about the future, not even wanting something very, very strongly. There is a magical side to us that secretly believes that if we wish something strongly enough, it will come true, as if wishing has some special power. This is one reason our desires become so strong: We believe in them. We believe that our desires have some ability to make our dreams come true.

Our desires are not powerful at all. Instead, desiring weakens us because our attention is on thoughts instead of what's coming out of the mystery, out of the moment, right now. Perhaps Essence is trying to co-create something wonderful with us, but Essence can't get our attention because we are dreaming about something else. This happens all the time actually, and Essence waits patiently for the opportunity to present its intentions and agenda. Sometimes Essence gets through, and sometimes it doesn't. Many people structure their lives according to the ego's dreams and desires, without realizing that another more fulfilling life is possible. Essence allows us to follow the ego's desires because that is one way we learn about being creators.

To discover what Essence intends, we have to fall in love with not knowing and with the quiet and stillness in which Essence appears and communicates. As long as we want to know, we will be in the grasp of the ego because the egoic mind pretends to know or promises knowing even when knowing isn't possible. And as long as we are in denial about the fact that we don't know, we will turn to the egoic mind for answers and believe that it has them because we want to believe it does.

We want to know so badly that we pretend we can know things we can't. We join the ego's world of make-believe, where our dreams and fantasies about the future seem real and important. We try to squeeze some juice out of our dreams and fantasies, but they always disappoint us because they are only ideas. Ideas may entertain us for a while, but they never satisfy us. Only what is real can satisfy us, and to experience reality, we have to move out of the mind and into the moment and stay in the moment long enough to experience what is real.

We are programmed to want to know, and we are programmed to believe the ego, so we have to remind ourselves we don't know and can't know whenever we find ourselves trying to know or pretending to know. This tendency to want to know and to pretend to know has to be seen again and again before it loosens and we begin to accept that we don't know. Then it may still be a while before we actually fall in love with not knowing, before we actually see that true knowing comes out of that space that seems so empty of knowing. We learn to listen to the Stillness and wait to catch knowing when it does arise. This is a very new way of living, and this way of being takes some time to get used to before it becomes second nature.

Wanting to know something before it's time to know keeps us in a state of discontentment. No matter how good our circumstances are, if we are wanting something, even just wanting to know something, this can keep us from being happy and grateful. Since the ego always wants to know but is unable to, it is never content with what it does know. It focuses on what it doesn't know and remains discontent.

One way out of this discontentment and frustration is to appreciate what we do know. What do you know for certain to be true right now? Do you know that the sun is shining (or not)? Do you know that you are breathing? Do you know that you feel relaxed (or tense)? Focusing on what we do know brings us into the moment and out of our mind, where we can feel some relief from the ego's discontentment and the drive to know.

Gratitude for what we do know can be extended to what we don't know. Yes, you can also be grateful for what you don't know. Essence loves the unknown, and when we are aligned with Essence, we are in touch with Essence's appreciation of life as it is. Not knowing is juicy and exciting. The ego doesn't focus on the deliciousness of not knowing, but that deliciousness is there. Not knowing makes life interesting: What's going to happen next? When we don't take life so personally, waiting to see what will happen next is exciting.

Appreciating the unknown requires a certain degree of surrender that the ego isn't capable of. The ego is all about control, which is why the ego suffers so. It tries to control what it can't control. The ego doesn't accept (surrender to) the fact that it isn't in control of life. When we surrender to this fact, we can enjoy the ride that life is taking us on. Essence is co-creating this life with us. We can give Essence more of the reins and enjoy the ride, or we can try to take the reins ourselves and not enjoy it. Surrender is really only giving up the control that we never had in the first place. Surrender is just admitting we never were in control. So relax, and enjoy what happens next. You can be sure that something will.

Exercise: Falling in Love with Not Knowing

Notice all the things you don't know: You don't know that the sun will rise tomorrow. You don't know that you will be alive even another hour or another minute. You don't know what will happen. And yet you assume a lot about life. Such assumptions keep you out of touch with the truth that there is an alive mystery here, unfolding unpredictably. What fun! Notice how the mind assumes it knows what is going to happen, not only in the next moment, but also tomorrow, next week, even next year. This is how the mind keeps us out of the freshness of the moment.

Wanting Growth More Than Ease and Comfort

Everything that happens to us that we don't like brings growth. When we find ourselves in a difficult or stressful situation, we learn things that cause us to change our behavior for the better. Sometimes we learn practical things: Your car gets a flat tire, and you learn how to change it or how important good tires are or any number of other things. Maybe you learn that other people can be very helpful in such situations. Every difficult situation is a potential catalyst for growth. Difficulties force us to find the place within us (Essence) that can accept and tolerate the difficulty. We can't have an experience, especially a difficult one, that doesn't entail some growth.

Life changes us, and sometimes it changes us dramatically. Dramatic change usually requires dramatic events. That's just the way it is. Ease and comfort have their place, but they don't catalyze growth like pain, difficulty, and loss do. These cause us to dig deep and develop resources we may never have realized we had. Ease and comfort usually don't do that, although they do provide respite from challenges and difficulties. Like breathing out and breathing in, ease and comfort provide balance to the tumultuousness of life. But when ease and comfort aren't happening and difficulties are, we have to learn to love growth more than we love ease and comfort, or we will suffer.

Loving growth is the key to getting through difficult times. We don't have to love the situation we find ourselves in, but if we want to get through it more gracefully and grow from it, we have to accept it—accept that this is the way things are for now. Acceptance isn't something the ego does, however. Acceptance is Essence's domain. It comes from Essence. When we accept something, we become aligned with Essence, and then we are able to experience Essence's patience, love, peace, wisdom, and clarity. Acceptance allows us to tap into these qualities, which can help us through the challenge. Resistance, anger, blame, bitterness, and other negative emotions, on the other hand, cut us off from the acceptance, wisdom, insight, and fuller perspective of Essence, which make it possible for us to navigate more gracefully through difficult times and grow from them.

Crises and difficulties can either further entrench us in the ego or drop us into Essence. If we become more entrenched in the ego, we suffer even more, while if we drop into Essence, we stop suffering. Essence is the way out of suffering. Regardless of what is happening, Essence's love, peace, acceptance, wisdom, and clarity are always available if we are willing to turn our attention to them.

Exercise: Telling Essence's Version of the Story

Think of a difficult time you went through. What is the story you tell about that time? How does it feel to tell this story? Do you feel sad, angry, guilty, hateful, or regretful? If the story you are telling causes you to feel contracted and bad about yourself, someone else, or life, then you aren't telling the whole story. The whole story would include what good came out of the situation, what you learned from it, how it changed you for the better, and what you discovered about yourself. That is the story Essence would tell. See how you feel when you tell that story.

Wanting What Is More Than What Isn't

We can go through anything with equanimity if we accept it. Doing this isn't easy initially. When we first experience a loss or difficulty, fear kicks in and we find ourselves immersed in the ego, its rejection and denial, its negative thoughts and feelings, and its attempts at problem-solving. Not accepting something produces all sorts of negative emotions: fear, anger, hatred, self-pity, blame, judgments, resentment, revenge, and jealousy. When the ego is challenged, it is at its worst, and the suffering can be immense.

The immensity of the suffering that being identified with the ego causes often motivates us to find other ways of coping than the ego's ways. We may be fortunate enough to encounter people who encourage us to accept our situation, which can move us into a different relationship to it and make other qualities of Essence available to us.

What often interferes with acceptance is a simple misunderstanding: We assume that we have to like something to accept it. But accepting something just means letting it be the way it is (as if we actually have any other choice!). Being unwilling to have the experience we are having is what causes us to suffer. When we push away or try to avoid or deny the experience we are having, we suffer; when we embrace the experience we are having, we stop suffering.

The ego resists loss and difficulties with all its might because the ego fears challenges. The ego's fear turns a challenging experience into something that's hard to bear. Fear takes us out of the moment and into the ego's world, where dreams just as easily become nightmares. The truth is, even in the most challenging moments, love, peace, joy, acceptance, and excitement about life are present, at least subtly. These positive feeling states coexist with the pain, sadness, anger, and fear the ego produces. During difficult times, we are challenged to discover these positive feeling states instead of following the ego into its world.

Essence can bear anything because Essence loves life and because it can find love in any moment. Not only is love alive within us, but it is also evident all around us: The sun shines, people care, we are breathing, life is still happening. The ego creates a different experience of life than this when it doesn't like what's happening: It narrows our attention down onto the negative feeling or negative story we are telling ourselves, which magnifies and deepens our suffering and may prevent us from seeing a solution. The ego frightens and angers us with its stories, until our situation seems unbearable and unsolvable.

Essence, on the other hand, makes challenging situations bearable by expanding our awareness to include all of what's happening, not just what we don't want to be happening, but good things that are also true about the moment, including the presence of courage, kindness, optimism, and love. This expansion of awareness also allows for insight and wisdom, which not only help us cope with the challenge, but also may provide a solution.

Accepting a challenging situation is much easier when half of the story isn't left out. The ego excludes so much in its stories. It overlooks the growth, love, understanding, and compassion that can come from a challenge. When the ego doesn't get what it wants, it paints the picture black. The ego doesn't see that even the worst events and circumstances have beauty and value for us. In part, overlooking the whole truth happens because the whole truth isn't always immediately apparent—and may never be. However, if we try, we can find positives in any experience, even in the midst of it. When we view a challenging situation from Essence's perspective instead of from the ego's, acceptance is much easier.

Our challenges are particularly hard to accept if we feel they have no value. When they are felt to have value, they become easier to accept, and we don't suffer over them so much. The difference between suffering and not suffering over something is our point of view, not so much whether what is happening is what we want or don't want. Acceptance is the willingness to let things be the way they are because we trust that our difficulties are serving us and serving life in some way, even if we don't know how they are serving. If we are willing to trust that our difficulties have some value, we are more likely to experience them as valuable and discover the value they do have.

Acceptance requires some humility. Although we may not know why we are having the experience we are having, we trust that something wiser than us does know and cares enough to have designed, or allowed, it to serve our growth. Unlike the ego, we are willing to submit to an Intelligence that may know more than we do about what is necessary for our growth and for the good of the Whole. While the ego claims to know what is good or bad (based on what it wants and doesn't want), we humbly admit we don't know why some things are the way they are, and we understand we may not even be meant to know. The mystery keeps some secrets from us.

Wanting Gratitude More Than Desiring

Gratitude is a quality of Essence, and feeling and expressing gratitude aligns us with Essence. All that is needed to align with Essence is to recognize that gratitude is already here. Do you feel even a sliver of gratitude for life, for being, for moving, for breathing, for feeling, for thinking, for seeing, for hearing? Whatever is happening is a reason for gratitude. Essence is grateful simply for the opportunity to be alive, and we feel that gratitude too when we pay attention to the subtle gratitude that exists in every moment.

Gratitude is felt as joy, but that joy may be only very subtly experienced until we pay attention to it, and then it becomes stronger and more obvious. Paying attention to gratitude or to anything else requires the will to do that. What we give our attention to is a choice. The funny thing about attention is that we can only give our attention fully to one thing at a time, and what we give it to is what we identify with. What we give our attention to is what we are choosing in that moment and therefore what we are desiring.

Many say they want love, but are they giving their attention to love or to a sense of lacking love? When we say we want something, we must feel we lack it, or why would we want it? We don't want things we already have or things that are already here, only things we perceive as not being here. If we want love, peace, joy, and contentment, we only have to recognize that they are already here. They are qualities of who we really are and have always been here. If we want something like money, beauty, or success, we only have to recognize that it is only our ideas that keep us from feeling rich, beautiful, or successful, since these only exist as concepts within the mind. What are you telling yourself that is keeping you from experiencing that you already have enough wealthy, success, and beauty? If you felt you had enough of these, it would be easy to feel grateful. Gratitude is the natural result of being aligned with Essence because then we realize that nothing is lacking or needed to be completely content. That is truly the definition of being rich.

We all have plenty to be grateful for. Feeling gratitude is just a matter of putting our attention on what we do have instead of on what we don't have. The ego sees lack, and Essence owns all that is. Essence knows itself as everything and is therefore lacking nothing. Moreover, Essence isn't fooled by the ego's assumption that some experience or some thing can make us happy. If we aren't already happy, having some experience or getting something won't change that. This is an essential truth the ego refuses to believe: Happiness lies within. Happiness isn't something to be sought, but something that is already present.

Seeking is what the ego does. It seeks because it assumes a position of lack. It desires because it sees what isn't here instead of what is here. Furthermore, it desires what isn't here more than what is here. To experience desire and lack, the ego has to deny or discount what's here. The ego focuses on what isn't here by creating an ideal image or fantasy of a moment (one without any negatives) that is very different from the present moment. The ego compares its perfect fantasy with its *idea* of the current reality, which leaves out much of what is true about the current reality, such as the positives. In this way, the ego builds a case for rejecting what is. The ego rejects everything about what is because it doesn't like some of what is.

In this world of duality, finding something we don't like about whatever is happening is easy. The ego focuses on what it doesn't like, as if this is a fair and complete picture of what is happening, and then offers solutions for improving the situation. This is how the ego keeps us involved with it: It points out what is wrong and then offers ideas for how to make things better. This keeps us very busy, sometimes for lifetimes.

Gratitude is the antidote to desire. While desire sees lack, gratitude sees abundance. Desiring is a subtle way of complaining about what is, while gratitude is rejoicing in what is. These are very different states of consciousness. Which state would you prefer to live in? We always have a choice. Because desiring is our default position, it's easy to desire, while being grateful takes awareness and a willingness to be grateful. Finding the place of gratitude and staying there is much more difficult than complaining because, for one thing, it means we have much less to do!

If you didn't have your desires to run after, what would you do? If you were satisfied with life as it is, what would you do? The ego considers contentment dangerous because the ego equates contentment with being lazy. Besides, the ego can't exist in the state of gratitude. It disappears when we drop into the moment. When we are present in the moment and experiencing the gratitude that naturally arises from the moment, the ego is defunct, useless, out of a job. The ego loses all significance.

Because the ego can't coexist with gratitude, gratitude can change your life. Gratitude can change what you do and how you do things. Who would think that something as simple as gratitude could be so powerful? The ego's existence is built on steering us away from this amazing force that is at the core of our being. Gratitude is the ongoing experience of Essence, and it's powerfully transformative. Gratitude can transform us from an unhappy person to a happy one, from a selfish person to a loving one, and from a restless person to a peaceful one. It turns out that gratitude feels much better than desiring. Being grateful is a much better choice than desiring, but not necessarily an easier one.

Exercise: Experiencing Gratitude

What are you grateful for? We take so much for granted. Life provides so much, we accept what it offers and then hold out our hand for more, wondering where the next goodie will come from and when it's going to get here, without appreciating the bounty that is already here. We aren't here on this earth for long, and in the end, everything is taken from us. The point isn't to get more things and better things, but to enjoy what is in our life right now because this moment will never come again.

Happiness Is a State of Not Desiring

When are you the happiest — when you are wanting something or not? Happiness and desiring can't coexist because desiring is an assumption that something is missing, and what can be happy about that? We think we enjoy desiring, but do we really? Through fantasizing, we like to pretend we already have what we desire. But what is better—having what you want or having a fantasy about that? Desiring creates a sense of lack when there's no reason to feel lack, and fantasies reinforce that sense of lack.

The present moment is exactly as it is meant to be. What is missing in it? The ego's answer to that question is, "A lot," but is that true? Are you going to take the ego's word for it? When we are aligned with Essence, nothing has changed about whatever is happening, but suddenly everything seems just fine the way it is. If you have had even one moment like this, you know that many more moments could be like this. Nothing changed to cause this transformation but your state of consciousness. You changed your mind or, more accurately, you moved out of your mind and into your Heart, where it's possible to feel that the moment is exactly right, for now.

Every moment is completely unique, and it isn't long before one moment changes into another. We are participants in each moment, but we aren't creating it, nor do we have the power to change it. It's already too late for that. Our choices do shape the next moment to some extent, but so much else that is beyond our control is appearing in every moment and shaping it that we can hardly assume we are central to that shaping. And yet that is the ego's attitude. The ego assumes it can control and change reality and that its desires are an adequate reason to do that. This is egocentric and unrealistic, and it's good to see this. Once we see this, we can relax and stop trying so hard to change things according to our will.

There's a greater will at work here, much more powerful than the ego's will. This greater will is making life happen all around us, and we are only a small part of the ever-moving, ever-changing experience that we call the moment. We can stand in awe of the moment, play in it, and rejoice in it. Or we can lament that it's not the moment we wanted, as the ego does. The ego's relationship to the moment is ludicrous, although the ego doesn't see it that way. Fortunately, we are able to separate ourselves from the ego's point of view and align ourselves with this great will. What a blessing it is to see the truth, and what a burden it has been to try to control, change, and fix this blessed moment. Once we are done with trying to do that, we can begin to enjoy the moment just the way it is.

It is really possible to enjoy life no matter what is happening because the only one here who isn't enjoying life is the ego. There is something else that is enjoying life immensely, and you are That! The secret that happiness lies within is the secret that you are that which is happy, has always been happy, and will always be happy. The only thing that has ever kept you from seeing this is the ego. Now that you know you are not the ego, how the ego sees things doesn't matter. Let it complain, judge, desire, fantasize, fear, doubt, and try to cause problems. The ego is like a lunatic in the attic that you can just ignore. Its judgments, complaints, fears, fantasies, and desires don't have to be yours anymore. They never really were yours. They were just the conditioning you were given.

The more you stop listening to the egoic mind, the more you realize just how unnecessary it is. However, you have to trust this enough to stop listening to that aspect of the mind, and that can take time. The loosening of our attachment to the egoic mind is usually a slow and gradual process, although at times this process can unfold very fast. Of greatest importance in this process is the willingness to question the egoic mind and to not believe it. You question what it tells you until you are convinced that it has nothing of value to say. Eventually, you get to the point where as soon as you hear the ego's voice, you ignore it and put your attention elsewhere.

Even after dismissing most of your thoughts, there will still be some thoughts that seem like your own voice and not the ego's. Those are the thoughts you are still identified with, the ones you still believe. When you agree with some thought and speak it, that's an opportunity to question that thought. The conditioning you still give voice to is the conditioning that still needs to be seen. So you ask: "Is that thought really true?" You may find that when you speak those thoughts, they feel false or hollow, like they lack solidity and truth. This is a sign that you don't really believe those thoughts anymore, and eventually, you will be done speaking those too.

This process of seeing through and detaching from the egoic mind usually goes on for quite some time, even years, because most of us have considerable conditioning that needs to be seen and dissolved. This process needs to be accepted, and it can't be rushed. If you don't accept the slowness of this process, you will find yourself contracted and suffering over your progress. The ego will berate you for not being more enlightened, if you let it. This judgment on the part of the ego is one more thing to be seen.

Loving Your Desires

Our desires are not the enemy, and if we resist them, we will remain caught in ego identification. Our desires do have to be seen for what they are, however, or moving beyond them will be difficult. We are naturally evolving from being driven by the ego's desires to being driven by Essence, which has always been driving us to some extent. As we evolve, Essence becomes a bigger player in our life, and we identify with the egoic mind less and less. Suffering naturally decreases as our identification with it weakens.

Essence loves. It doesn't reject anything. Acceptance is a form of love, and acceptance is Essence's way of loving. Essence accepts. It even accepts the ego and its desires. Any lack of acceptance we may feel for the ego or for its desires comes from the ego, and that lack of acceptance will keep us tied to the ego. Whenever we find ourselves rejecting a desire, that's the ego in spiritual clothing, trying to get us to comply with its ideas of what it is to be spiritual. By accepting the ego's desires instead of rejecting them, we drop into Essence, where we can experience the real force that is driving and shaping our life.

Essence is fine with the ego's desires. When we are aligned with Essence, we allow desire to be there, but we don't give it the power to shape our lives. We accept and allow the ego's desires because they are part of life, part of the grand design. To be free from desire, all we have to do is stop giving the ego's desires the power to structure our life. To be free from the suffering they cause, all we have to see is that those desires don't bring us happiness. How funny it is that we give desire the power to shape our lives. We really believe our desires — until we don't. We aren't used to examining them or our other thoughts. But once we do, the game changes. Then it's possible to discover what else is here and what has always been here.

ABOUT the AUTHOR

Gina Lake is the author of over twenty books about awakening to one's true nature, including *From Stress to Stillness, All Grace, In the World but Not of It, The Jesus Trilogy, A Heroic Life, Trusting Life, Embracing the Now, Radical Happiness,* and *Choosing Love.* She is also a gifted intuitive with a master's degree in counseling psychology and over twenty-five years' experience supporting people in their spiritual growth. Her website offers information about her books and online course, a free ebook, a blog, and audio and video recordings:

www.RadicalHappiness.com

Awakening Now Online Course

It's time to start living what you've been reading about. Are you interested in delving more deeply into the teachings in Gina Lake's books, receiving ongoing support for waking up, and experiencing the power of Christ Consciousness transmissions? You'll find that and much more in the Awakening Now online course:

This course was created for your awakening. The methods presented are powerful companions on the path to enlightenment and true happiness. Awakening Now will help you experience life through fresh eyes and discover the delight of truly being alive. This 100-day inner workout is packed with both time-honored and original practices that will pull the rug out from under your ego and wake you up. You'll immerse yourself in materials, practices, guided meditations, and inquiries that will transform your consciousness. And in video webinars, you'll receive transmissions of Christ Consciousness. These transmissions are a direct current of love and healing that will accelerate your evolution and help you break through to a new level of being. By the end of 100 days, you will have developed new habits and ways of being that will result in being more richly alive and present and greater joy and equanimity.

www.RadicalHappiness.com/online-courses

More Books by Gina Lake

Available in paperback, ebook, and audiobook formats.

A Heroic Life: New Teachings from Jesus on the Human Journey. The hero's journey—this human life—is a search for the greatest treasure of all: the gifts of your true nature. These gifts are your birthright, but they have been hidden from you, kept from you by the dragon: the ego. These gifts are the wisdom, love, peace, courage, strength, and joy that reside at your core. *A Heroic Life* shows you how to overcome the ego's false beliefs and face the ego's fears. It provides you with both a perspective and a map to help you successfully and happily navigate life's challenges and live heroically. This book is another in a series of books dictated to Gina Lake by Jesus.

Living in the Now: How to Live as the Spiritual Being That You Are. The 99 essays in *Living in the Now* will help you realize your true nature and live as that. They answer many questions raised by the spiritual search and offer wisdom on subjects such as fear, anger, happiness, aging, boredom, desire, patience, forgiveness, acceptance, love, commitment, meditation, being present, emotions, trusting your Heart, and many other deep subjects. These essays will help you become more conscious, present, happy, loving, grateful, at peace, and fulfilled.

All Grace: New Teachings from Jesus on the Truth About Life. Grace is the mysterious and unseen movement of God upon creation, which is motivated by love and indistinct from love. *All Grace* was given to Gina Lake by Jesus and represents his wisdom and understanding of life. It is about the magnificent and incomprehensible force behind life, which created life, sustains it, and operates within it as you and me and all of creation. *All Grace* is full of profound and life-changing truth.

From Stress to Stillness: Tools for Inner Peace. Most stress is created by how we think about things. *From Stress to Stillness* will help you to examine what you are thinking and change your relationship to your thoughts so that they no longer result in stress. Drawing from the wisdom traditions, psychology, New Thought, and the author's own experience as a spiritual teacher and counselor, *From Stress to Stillness* offers many practices and suggestions that will lead to greater peace and equanimity, even in a busy and stress-filled world.

In the World but Not of It: New Teachings from Jesus on Embodying the Divine: From the Introduction, by Jesus: "What I have come to teach now is that you can embody love, as I did. You can become Christ within this human life and learn to embody all that is good within you. I came to show you the beauty of your own soul and what is possible as a human. I came to show you that it is possible to be both human and divine, to be love incarnate. You are equally both. You walk with one foot in the world of form and another in the Formless. This mysterious duality within your being is what this book is about." This book is another in a series of books dictated to Gina Lake by Jesus.

Radical Happiness: A Guide to Awakening provides the keys to experiencing the happiness that is ever-present and not dependent on circumstances. This happiness comes from realizing that who you think you are is not who you really are. *Radical Happiness* describes the nature of the egoic state of consciousness and how it interferes with happiness, what awakening and enlightenment are, and how to live in the world after awakening.

The Jesus Trilogy. In this trilogy by Jesus, are three jewels, each shining in its own way and illuminating the same truth: You are not only human but divine, and you are meant to flourish and love one another. In words that are for today, Jesus speaks intimately and directly to the reader of the secrets to peace, love, and happiness. He explains the deepest of all mysteries: who you are and how you can live as he taught long ago. The three books in *The Jesus Trilogy* were dictated to Gina Lake by Jesus and include *Choice and Will, Love and Surrender,* and *Beliefs, Emotions, and the Creation of Reality.*

Embracing the Now: Finding Peace and Happiness in What Is. The Now—this moment—is the true source of happiness and peace and the key to living a fulfilled and meaningful life. *Embracing the Now* is a collection of essays that can serve as daily reminders of the deepest truths. Full of clear insight and wisdom, *Embracing the Now* explains how the mind keeps us from being in the moment, how to move into the Now and stay there, and what living from the Now is like. It also explains how to overcome stumbling blocks to being in the Now, such as fears, doubts, misunderstandings, judgments, distrust of life, desires, and other conditioned ideas that are behind human suffering.

Getting Free: Moving Beyond Negativity and Limiting Beliefs. To a large extent, healing our conditioning involves changing our relationship to our mind and discovering who we really are. *Getting Free* will help you do that. It will also help you reprogram your mind; clear negative thoughts and self-images; use meditation, prayer, forgiveness, and gratitude; work with spiritual forces to assist healing and clear negativity; and heal entrenched issues from the past.

Choosing Love: Moving from Ego to Essence in Relationships. Having a truly meaningful relationship requires choosing love over your conditioning, that is, your ideas, fantasies, desires, images, and beliefs. *Choosing Love* describes how to move beyond conditioning, judgment, anger, romantic illusions, and differences to the experience of love and oneness with another. It explains how to drop into the core of your Being, where Oneness and love exist, and be with others from there.

Trusting Life: Overcoming the Fear and Beliefs That Block Peace and Happiness. Fear and distrust keep us from living the life we were meant to live, and they are the greatest hurdles to seeing the truth about life—that it is good, abundant, supportive, and potentially joyous. *Trusting Life* is a deep exploration into the mystery of who we are, why we suffer, why we don't trust life, and how to become more trusting. It offers tools for overcoming the fear and beliefs that keep us from falling in love with life.

For more information, please visit the "Books" page at

www.RadicalHappiness.com

Manufactured by Amazon.ca
Bolton, ON

13470105R00099